Going Beyond Words

Also by Lois Huey-Heck

The Spirituality of Art
with Jim Kalnin

The Spirituality of Sex
with Mike Schwartzentruber, Mary Millerd,
and Charlotte Jackson

All author royalties are donated to Emerging Christian Way Media Society, a not-for-profit organization that seeks to give greater voice to a Christianity that is grounded in ancient and enduring practice and truth and is also alive and awake to the new thing God is doing.

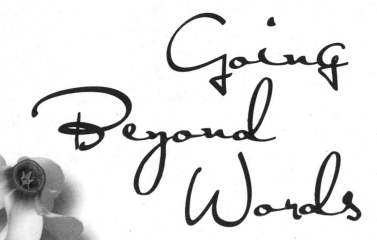

LOIS HUEY-HECK

Going Beyond Words

10 PRACTICES
FOR SPIRITUAL UNFOLDING

Editor: Ellen Turnbull
Cover and interior design: Chaunda Daigneault
Proofreader: Dianne Greenslade

CopperHouse is an imprint of Wood Lake Publishing, Inc. Wood Lake Publishing
acknowledges the financial support of the Government of Canada, through the Book
Publishing Industry Development Program (BPIDP) for its publishing activities. Wood
Lake Publishing also acknowledges the financial support of the Province of British
Columbia through the Book Publishing Tax Credit.

At Wood Lake Publishing, we practise what we publish, being guided by a concern
for fairness, justice, and equal opportunity in all of our relationships with employees
and customers. Wood Lake Publishing is committed to caring for the environment
and all creation. Wood Lake Publishing recycles, reuses, and encourages readers to
do the same. Resources are printed on 100% post-consumer recycled paper and
more environmentally friendly groundwood papers (newsprint), whenever possible. A
percentage of all profit is donated to charitable organizations.

Library and Archives Canada Cataloguing in Publication

Huey-Heck, Lois, 1957-
Going beyond words : 10 practices for spiritual unfolding / Lois Huey-Heck.

Accompanied by a CD.
Includes bibliographical references.
ISBN 978-1-55145-589-1

1. Spirituality. 2. Spiritual life.
3. Self-realization--Religious aspects. I. Title.

BL624.H83 2010   204'.4   C2010-905320-6

Published by CopperHouse
An imprint of Wood Lake Publishing Inc.
9590 Jim Bailey Road, Kelowna, BC, Canada, V4V 1R2
www.woodlakebooks.com
250.766.2778

Printing 10 9 8 7 6 5 4 3 2 1
Printed in Canada by
Transcontinental

Image credits:
cover (footprints)
  iStockphoto © DNY59
cover, pages 3, 7, 11, 17, 24,
  30, 37, 41, 48, 66, 81, 95,
  105, 113, 120, 121, 126
  (cyclamen) iStockphoto
  © marlies plank
pages 15, 22, 27, 35, 39,
  45, 63, 78, 102, 112
  iStockphoto
  © Maria Brzostowska
pages 9, 10, 16, 23, 28, 36,
  40, 46, 64, 79, 93, 103
  iStockphoto
  © Evelin Elmest
pages 21, 34, 52–60, 67, 121
  © Lois Huey-Heck

Contents

DEDICATION

For Jim (Feather) Kalnin
friend, wisdom-teacher, and lover

For all the seekers and finders ~
to paraphrase Carl Jung, "to be on the way
is to be at the destination."

ACKNOWLEDGEMENTS

John O'Donohue tells a story of a monk/seeker who understood that there was something to learn from everyone. He travelled around, intentionally learning from the one who was best at this, and then another who was best at that. He learned from everyone.

That much humility and grace I would also aspire to. Certainly this book is the result of countless encounters, some now beyond conscious memory. I have been blessed with an amazing communion of mentors, teachers, and encouragers, some of whom I've actually met. Their voices and teachings are woven in, around, and through this small book, and I pray I have done their teachings some small justice. The inspiration is theirs; any errors or gaps are mine.

To my spiritual director Carol Stokes, thanks for your wisdom, faithfulness, and even for blessed unrest. Heartfelt thanks to my earlier spiritual directors Patricia Baker and Tim Scorer, and spiritual mentors Granma Huey (who taught me about Mystery), Kathi Bentall, Donna Scorer, Ralph Milton, Bev Milton, Marilyn Perry, Donna Sinclair, Jim Taylor, the faithful creative teams for *The Whole People of God* and *Seasons of the Spirit*, John and Mary Robertson, Marion and Jack Best, and a Sunday school teacher from Trinity United Church in Vernon, BC, who said in 1966 that she did not believe in a literal hell. I was nine – it had an impact!

Thank you to my friends and former colleagues at Wood Lake Publishing. We have shared much. You have all taught me things (some lessons were more fun than others!). Although you are too many to name individually, please know that you have my sincere thanks and my affection for all the ways our working together nourished and stretched me.

To the members of Winfield United Church, my home congregation (remember me?), thanks for making me welcome even with my itinerant schedule.

To the community of Naramata Centre, which has been forming me in faith for almost thirty years, thanks seems such a small word. I owe you my life.

The staff and participants of the Pacific Jubilee Program have been another deeply formative community of learning and discovery for me. Thanks all of you, including current colleagues Don Grayston, Dawn Kilarski, Murray Groom, Miguel Perez-Gibson, and Ingrid Haus. The Spirit blows strongly through the Jubilee training programs for spiritual directors and I owe you my avocation.

There are specific parts of this project that would not have been possible without the following people: Mary Millerd (breath, visualization and energy work); Grainger Brown (absolute grace and encouragement); Hajime Naka (Tai Ji and Qigong); Dawn Kilarski (practice of presence, for compassion, and wisdom); Don Grayston (divina of dreams, Jubilee vision, radical support); Dorrie Petty (the process of wax-resist painting); John Pulfer (music and recording); Chris Duggan, Genevra Cavanagh, and Michael Martin (chants). To all of you, named and unnamed, may your part of the Great Work continue to bless you as much as it blesses the rest of us.

I want to say thank you, Ellen Turnbull, for believing in this project, for doing such a sensitive and skillful job of the editing, and for participating in both the text and the audio portions of this project. Your affirmation, patience, and support have been profoundly encouraging and have made this little project shine.

The last thank you today goes to all the people I've met in the ministry of spiritual direction. I hardly have words to express to you what a blessing it is that you have trusted me with your sacred stories. It is at once the most uplifting and the most humbling experience I know. You teach me another level of communion. God bless you.

Going Beyond Words

In our quest for God, we think too much, reflect too much, talk
too much. Even when we look at the dance we call creation,
we are all the time thinking, talking (to ourselves and others),
reflecting, analyzing, philosophizing. Words. Noise.
Be silent and contemplate the Dance. Just look. A star, a flower, a
fading leaf, a bird, a stone – any fragment of the Dance will do...
– Anthony de Mello

INTRODUCTION

Begin

Spirituality is the art of transfiguration.
— John O'Donohue
ANAM CARA

ohn O'Donohue's definition of spirituality is my all-time favourite illumination of spirituality, a word with a diverse range of interpretations. In five words, O'Donohue has summed up its power and potential. In five words, he has distilled a universe of possibility.

WHY

Spirituality as the art of transfiguration is for me the "why bother" of spiritual practice. It's the promise and challenge of our living spiritual traditions. All of them at their core are about the transformation/transfiguration of life. Of self into Self, of life yearning towards Life, and Life yearning back.

O'Donohue's definition says that the essence of spirituality is to be born anew. And that's not just once. In her book *The Body Has Its Reasons*, Therese Bertherat writes, *To be is never to cease being born.* Yes, and it bears repeating. *To be is never to cease being born.*

TRANSFIGURATION

Transfigure: ...*to transform... somebody or something, revealing great beauty, spirituality, or magnificence...*

Transform: to change something dramatically...to change somebody or something completely, especially improving their appearance or usefulness; to undergo total change... to change completely for the better; to convert something to different energy... to convert one form of energy to another.

– Excerpts from an online dictionary

I've written elsewhere about how I have seen the effect of transfiguration right at home. My life partner Jim (Feather) loves being outdoors. Given the choice he will always elect to be outside.

One of his favourite ways of communing with the natural world is to fly-fish from a small inflatable. His inflatable tube is propelled by his neoprene-covered legs and flippered feet as he sits just above lake level. No matter what the fishing is like and no matter what the weather, when he comes down off the mountain at the end of the day his eyes sparkle, his face shines, and he radiates joy. No matter if the fishing has been "good" or not, he glows. He is transfigured. For him, being in the water, feeling the wind on his face, and watching the patterns of light shine off riffles on the water is heartening, restorative, and healing. I never resent his time in nature. It nourishes his creative and generous spirit. It feeds him so that he not only has more joy and satisfaction in his own life, but he also has more to share with the world.

ART

O'Donohue was an author who chose his words with great care. Defining spirituality as "art" reflects a mature understanding of the dynamic process of transfiguration. In art, as in life, there are few certainties, and both art and life become lifeless when they are reduced to formulas.

Certain amounts of scientific curiosity, observation, and inquiry are an asset. A measure of persistence[1] – a consistency of attentiveness and practice – is essential. Honouring our emotional, cognitive, and body intelligences (or in other words, "being whole") increases the potential for transformation. The willingness to maintain "beginner's mind" helps us stay open and receptive to Inspiration. A desire to serve and to give back creates a certain receptivity. These are some of the ways of art.

YIELD

Cynthia Bourgeault is a contemplative who leads retreats, teaches, and writes prolifically about the spiritual life. Her small book *The Wisdom Way of Knowing* includes a most basic and profound teaching on spiritual practice.

> …confronted by an outer threat or opportunity, you can notice yourself responding in one of two ways. Either you will brace, harden and resist, or you will soften, open and yield. If you go with the former gesture, you will be catapulted immediately into your smaller self…If you stay with the latter…you will remain in alignment with your innermost being, and through it divine being can reach you. Spiritual practice at its no-frills simplest is a moment by moment learning not to do any thing in a state of internal brace. Bracing is never worth the cost.

Jungian author Marion Woodman writes that our goal should not be the eradication of ego but rather the development of an ego which is mature, healthy, and flexible enough to surrender itself in service of the Divine. Surrender is not a popular concept in our culture but it's a foundation of mystical spiritual practice.

LOVE

In her book *Practicing Peace in Times of War* Pema Chodron tells a story from Jarvis Masters, a prisoner on death row. One night, Jarvis is reading by the light from the television in his cell. He has the sound turned off. Three times he looks up at the screen and calls out the question, "What's going on?" The first time the answer is that it is the Ku Klux Klan yelling and complaining. The second time it's Greenpeace folks demonstrating. The third time it's a U.S. Senator blaming the other party.

Chodron writes,

Jarvis starts laughing and he calls down, "I've learned something here tonight. Sometimes they're wearing Klan outfits, sometimes they're wearing Greenpeace outfits, sometimes they're wearing suits and ties, but they all have the same angry faces."

It echoes a wisdom my Aunt Merlin shared with me many years ago. I don't know the original source but I know the truth of it: *If it's not love, it's fear.*

I know that if I do not have love in my heart, mind, and body, I may be expressing anger, hurt, resentment, judgment, or aggression. Under it all, if it's not love, it's fear that's gotten hold of me.

Our friend John Pulfer has been meditating for years. Sometime during the second George Bush administration some friends were lamenting another horrendous policy of the administration. John didn't love the choices being taken any more than the rest of us, but he said something that has challenged and inspired me ever since. John told us that when he was meditating and praying in the mornings he was sending love to George Bush. Not in support of Bush's actions, but because John knows that love has infinitely more potential to create change and healing than criticism and hate could ever have.

PRACTICE

Contemplation, meditation, and prayer are some of the ways we "practice" our spirituality. Like learning new music on an instrument or drawing in a sketchbook, we mature as spiritual beings as we practice being present to *the* Presence. By slowing ourselves down (even for just a few minutes a day) and bringing our focus to that-which-is-bigger-than-us, we are transformed.

The practices in this book could all fall under the heading *the practice of presence.* It's the main event of spiritual practice. In terms of practice, everything else flows from this starting place "I am here, Beloved, present to You, myself, and all the others." And then we are transformed.

Science has recently discovered three startling new possibilities regarding how we think, feel, love, heal, and find meaning in our life. This research suggests that the heart thinks, cells remember, and that both of these processes are related to an as yet mysterious, extremely powerful, but very subtle energy with properties unlike any other known force. If the preliminary insights regarding these prospects continue to be verified, science may be taking the first tentative steps toward understanding more about what shamans, kahuna, priests, spiritual leaders, and healers from ancient traditional medicines have been teaching about for centuries — the energy of the human spirit and the coded information that is the human soul.

— Paul Pearsall

THE HEART'S CODE

---

1   When I was a student in the Pacific Jubilee Program,
    I lamented once to Don Grayston that my spiritual practice
    was not consistent. Don's wise counsel has stayed with me.
    He said he's found persistence to be a more helpful goal
    than consistency.

ONE
Presence

To see a World in a Grain of Sand,
And a Heaven in a Wild Flower,
Hold Infinity in the palm of your hand,
And Eternity in an hour.
— William Blake

Our sense of time is altered in moments of deep and intense
experience, so we know what that means. We feel at home in
that now, in that eternity, because that is the only place where
we really are. We cannot be in the future and we cannot be in the
past; we can only be in the present. We are only real to the extent
to which we are living in the present here and now.
— David Steindl-Rast
THE MUSIC OF SILENCE

At our first session, my then-new spiritual director Carol asked about my spiritual practice. I told her that my very best time for practice is early morning – before my monkey mind gets too revved up. My favourite practice, I told her, is embodied prayer. Embodied prayer can be mindful gestures, yoga, qigong, dance, or complex sacred movements. When my prayers are expressed in and through my body I am more fully in the present moment, less distracted, and more whole.

Carol asked why the movement is so important to me. I explained that I pray and meditate better when I remember that I live in a body, and when all of me is awake and present.

Carol persisted. "What makes the dancing a spiritual practice and not just exercise?" she asked.

Such a good question!

"It's the quality of presence," I answered. "It's about my intention to be present to the moment itself, to my own body and experience, and thereby to be as fully present to the Beloved as possible."

The world is full of interesting and not-so-interesting distractions. And I can be very distractible. When I am present, I am awake to wonder, discovery, and a sense of being part of the seamless Oneness.

The answer that arose in response to Carol's question has proven to be a good gauge. When I notice that my attention has wandered away from the grain of sand, the wildflower, or the person talking to me, I choose to breathe and centre and come back to the here and now. It's a practice in and of itself, and I watch my attention (as best I can) not only in focused times of spiritual practice but also dur-ing spiritual accompaniment, soulfriend-ing, and "casual" conversation, and while working, leading a group, painting, writing, driving…

A Practice of Presence 1

1 Sit comfortably in a chair with your feet flat on the floor/earth.

Observe your grounding to the earth by paying attention to your sitting bones and buttocks being supported by the chair you're in, and visualizing its connectedness to the ground. Be aware also of your connection to the earth through the soles of your feet.

Stay with this visualization until you *know* at both cognitive and physical-sensate levels that you are solidly supported in this moment – held to the earth by the pull of gravity.

Pause and enjoy this awareness.

2 Visualize a cord of light that starts at your tailbone and extends upwards along the vertebrae that channel your spinal cord. In your mind's eye, picture this cord continuing up and out through the top of your head and connecting you to the sky.

Allow this connection to the heavens to hold you upright, spine relaxed yet awake, in comfortable vertical alignment.

While experiencing this connection to sky, remember your relationship to earth.

3 Turn your attention to your breathing.

Without changing anything, become aware of the natural rhythm of your breath.

Notice the inhalation, pause, exhalation, pause…

As you notice the rhythm of your breathing, say to yourself, *I know I am breathing in*, and *I know I am breathing out*.

Rest in this sense of being held and supported between earth and sky.

Be mindful only of your breathing for a few complete cycles: inhalation, pause, exhalation, pause.

When/if you find your thoughts wandering, gently come back to observing your breath.

This practice can be done very slowly to give ample opportunity to sink ever more deeply into the awareness that you live in a body that is held and supported between heaven and earth, and that moment by moment, the gift of life enters the body through the breath. This practice can also be done for a few moments at a red light, at your desk, or in the midst of a challenging conversation or situation. The school of thought of Buddhist monk Thich Nhat Hahn encourages the practice of using a few "mindful" breaths at any time to bring us into the eternal *now*.

One of the seeming spiritual dichotomies is that the very fact of being fully present in the moment is what enables us, in Blake's words, to "hold infinity in the palm of your hand and eternity in an hour."

Now is the Time
Here is the Place
And this is Holy Ground

The music for this chant can be found in the resource section and on track 1 of the accompanying CD.

A Practice of Presence II

Donna Gruhlke and Dawn Kilarski developed the I AM HERE practice based on the Gurdjieff exercises and movements that provide opportunities for us to embody our spiritual work and re-integrate the parts of ourselves. I experience the I AM HERE as intention and affirmation, as prayer, and as blessing.

Three words:
I AM HERE.

Four gestures:

1 Hands resting in lap, palms down, eyes straight ahead in present time.

2 Hands form an open circle in front of the centre of the chest near the heart.

3 Arms and hands rise up: upper arms parallel with the ground, forearms upright, palms open to the sky, hands at right angles to the body, eyes skyward.

4 Arms cross with fingertips lightly touching your collarbones, eyes downward.

The same word won't always be with the same gesture (it's part of keeping us "awake" and present). A complete cycle (four repetitions of the words) brings us back to the starting point. Repeat as many times as possible. Keep bringing your attention back to the three words and four gestures — prayer, intention, and blessing. Dawn most often uses Cecil Lyttle's slow and evocative piano music as an accompaniment. This practice also works very well in silence.

TWO

Breath

One of the most ancient words for spirit is the Hebrew Ruah; this is also the word for air or wind...Ancient recognition links the wild creativity of the Spirit with the breath of the soul in the human person...At the deepest level, breath is sister of spirit.
    Then there's the relationship between breath and spirit – the intuition and/or wisdom that breath is connected to the movement of the spirit.

– John O'Donohue

ANAM CARA

Breathing superficially and irregularly becomes our most effective means of (controlling) our emotions, of suppressing our feelings.

– Therese Bertherat

THE BODY HAS ITS REASONS

An adult at rest breathes about 12–20 times per minute for a total of 17,280 to 28,800 breaths per day. Breathing is so familiar that we scarcely notice it, yet there's nothing more essential for maintaining life in these bodies than the intake and expiration of breath. Breath is an everyday miracle — the gift of life given moment by moment.

Energy worker, teacher, and spiritual director Mary Millerd reminds us, "We can't breathe in the past. We can't breathe in the future. We can only breathe in the present moment." This present-moment quality of breath is one of the things that make attention to breathing a powerful spiritual practice. Coincidentally, the present is the only dimension of time in which we can meet and be met by the fullness of our own selves, each other, and the Divine.

John O'Donohue writes, "Your breathing and the rhythm of your breathing can return you to your ancient belonging, 'to the house,' as Eckhardt says, 'that you never left, where you always live: the house of spiritual belonging.'"

A Breathing Practice

This practice expands conscious awareness of a single point (such as thought or emotion or physical sensation) to awareness of them all.

Begin with A *Practice of Presence* from page 18 or 21 and continue when ready.

Maintain the natural pace and depth of your breath during this practice.

1 Close your eyes and imagine your breath entering your body through the front of your rib cage.

With each *inhalation*, visualize the gift of life entering your chest area.

With each *exhalation*, visualize your life breath radiating out through and beyond your rib cage, creating spaciousness.

2 When you are ready, shift the path of your breath. As it enters your body through your chest wall, draw your breath down into your abdomen/belly.

With each *inhalation*, visualize the gift of life entering your chest and travelling down your spine.

With each *exhalation*, visualize your life-breath radiating out through and beyond your belly, creating spaciousness.

3 When you are ready, again shift the path of your breath. Visualize your breath entering your body through your belly and travelling all the way up your spine.

With each *inhalation*, visualize the gift of life entering your belly and travelling to the top of your spine.

With each *exhalation*, visualize your life breath radiating out through and beyond your head.

4 As you're ready, shift the pattern of your breathing again. This time visualize your breath coming in through the front of your forehead, down your spine and radiating out through your feeling centre in all directions. Be aware of the way breath nourishes your whole body.

With each *inhalation*, visualize the gift of life filling your whole being.

With each *exhalation*, visualize your life breath radiating out through your whole being.

5 When you have a sense of completion, let your breath return to its own natural rhythm. You may wish to offer some gratitude for the gift of life given in the breath.

Breathing

It is late
and I lie awake,
remembering.

I could fold into nostalgia
for the first boy I ever loved
for the first man I ever lay with
for moments lost
for if and if...

Instead
I place my hand, gently, on your chest
I watch your sleeping face
~ thinning hair spiking in tangled wisps
~soft wrinkles around your eyes and lips

You are not young
The wild beauty of our youth is a ragged memory

The moonlight,
    slanting through our bedroom window
    etches deep shadows under your eyes,
    glints off the grey in your beard,
        and tries to draw me
            into yearning for twenty or forty

The moonlight shines off the hematite stone
    I gave you for your forty-fifth birthday
    and shows me
        that all my love is now,
            breathing,
                under my hand.
                    — Marilyn Raymond

THREE
Whole-minded

This...is for those who are willing to respect the magnificence of the brain while considering that it is a remarkable partner with, but not the master over, the body and heart.

The heart considers itself part of a three-part Mind, made up of brain, body and heart, and it is ready to join with the rational power of the brain and the extraordinary sense of the body to make its soothing contribution to our daily living. While the brain uses its rational brilliance to seek reasons, the heart's wisdom teaches that the three-part Mind it is a part of can never get "its" way, only go with The Way.

– Paul Pearsall

THE HEART'S CODE

Wisdom is a way of knowing that goes beyond one's mind, one's rational understanding, and embraces the whole of a person: mind, heart and body. In many branches of the ancient Wisdom tradition, the human being is considered to be three-centered — or "three-brained," as G.I. Gurdjieff, the influential modern interpreter of the tradition, picturesquely describes it. The intellectual faculty, or the intelligence of the brain, is one way of knowing to be sure, but it is joined by two additional faculties: the intelligence of the "moving" center and the intelligence of the emotional center. These three centers must all be working, and working in harmony...

— Cynthia Bourgeault
THE WISDOM WAY OF KNOWING

If we are using one mind we are delusional. If we are using two minds we are semi-delusional... If we are using three minds we are waking up.

— Paraphrase of a quote attributed to George Gurdjieff

nowing that our wisdom and knowing come from more than our amazing brain has profound potential for our transfiguration. Sometimes called *three-mindedness,* this idea has been espoused by the Gurdjieff school, by Christian contemplatives and mystics such as Cynthia Bourgeault, and from a more scientific point of view by psychoneuroimmunologist Paul Pearsall in his book *The Heart's Code.* The descriptive language varies somewhat from source to source, but the understandings are remarkably similar: while our brain is powerful, it is not the only part of us that carries memory and has intelligence.

This can be a challenging idea for those of us in the one-third world where brain power is so highly regarded. It wasn't *always* like this, but from as far back as classical Greece (and further back in some of the severe esthetic schools of the East), the body and emotions were regarded as "lesser" than the brain, and even as sinful, base, and dangerous.

Thankfully, recent decades have seen a plethora of research confirming and reminding us that we are unified entities.

Not only is our brain not separate, but there is ongoing communication between all parts of ourselves, with each part affecting and being affected by the others. This understanding of our inner terrain echoes the "advancement" of our thinking right back into the wisdom of indigenous cultures and earth-based spiritualities that have always known we are more than our thinking minds.

The following practice builds on the breathing practice from chapter two. It

offers a way to honour our three-mindedness, and encourages collaboration between our centres of knowing.

A Wholeness Practice
Three-Mindedness

Maintain the natural pace and depth of
your breathing during this practice.

1 Close your eyes and imagine your breath entering your body through the front of
your rib cage. With each *inhalation*, visualize the gift of life entering your chest area.

With each *exhalation*, visualize your
life-breath radiating through and
beyond your rib cage.

Continue to visualize inhaling
through your chest wall and exhaling into the whole ribcage.

The rib bones that shelter lungs
and heart also provide a home for
our emotional intelligence – our
feeling self. Each breath you bring
into the feeling centre of the body
nourishes its wisdom.

Without changing anything – and
free of judgment – notice what
comes under your attention in this
part of your body.

- Is it easy or hard to bring breath, life, and spirit into your feeling centre?
- How much room is there for your exhalation?
- What size is the space?
- Is the space dense or open? Receptive or resistant?
- Does it have a colour? A shape?

- What feelings are you aware of in your emotional centre?

As you hold awareness of this part of your "knowing," what wants your attention?

With compassion, receive whatever arises.

2 When you are ready, shift the path of your breath. As it enters your body through your chest, draw your breath down into your abdomen/belly. With each *inhalation*, visualize the gift of life entering your chest and travelling down your spine.

With each *exhalation* visualize your life breath radiating through and beyond your belly.

The abdomen/gut/belly is largely where nutrients are assimilated to support life. Some Eastern thinking identifies the belly as the source of all movement. This part of us is also home to our "moving" or bodily intelligence – our kinesthetic/physical self. Each breath you bring into the moving centre of the body is nourishment for its wisdom.

Continue to visualize inhaling through your chest wall. Let the breath move down the spine and then exhale into the whole abdomen.

Without judging or changing anything, notice what comes under your attention in this part of your body.

o Is it easy or hard to bring breath, life, and spirit into your moving centre?
o Is there room for your exhalation?
o What size is the space?

o Is the space dense or open? Receptive or resistant?
o Does it have a colour? A shape?
o What physical sensation(s) are you aware of?

As you hold awareness of this part of your knowing, what wants your attention? With compassion, receive whatever arises.

3 When you are ready, again shift the path of your breath. Visualize your breath entering your body through your belly and travelling all the way up your spine. With each *inhalation*, visualize the gift of life entering your belly and travelling to the top of your spine.

With each *exhalation*, visualize your life breath radiating through and beyond your head.

The bones of the head surround and protect the brain, the source of our cognitive thinking and prob-

lem solving. This "thinking centre" also influences how we see and comprehend the world.

Continue to visualize inhaling through your belly and up the spine, and exhaling into your head.

Without judging or changing anything, notice what comes under your attention in this part of your body.

- Is it easy or hard to bring breath, life, and spirit into your thinking centre?
- Is there room for your exhalation?
- What size is the space?

- Is the space dense or open? Receptive or resistant?
- Does it have a colour?
- What thoughts are you aware of?

As you hold awareness of this part of your knowing, what wants your attention?

With compassion, receive whatever arises.

4 As you're ready, shift the pattern of your breathing again, visualizing your breath coming in through the front of your forehead and down into your emotional centre. Then visualize your exhalation flowing out in all directions, nourishing your whole body. Continue for several breaths.

5 Visualize your three centres of intelligence (feeling, moving and thinking) as well-rounded orbs in vertical alignment along your spine. If they are of equal size and are gently overlapping, simply continue to breathe into your three-minds and become familiar with your three centres of wisdom in right relationship with each other.

If you find that your three centres are not roughly equal in size and/or are not aligned vertically, continue to pay attention to your breathing and consciously bring your attention and life force to each centre. Right relationship may not come in your first session. This connection and alignment will also slip from time to time as we are pulled and pushed by the events of our lives and by our old patterns. When this happens, this practice can help you notice any imbalance and gently — with self-compassion and forgiveness — breathe the relationship back into well-being.

When you're finished for today, open your eyes, let your breath take its own pattern, and stroke your arms, legs, and face to bring your whole self back into the room.

When a person is poised in all three centers, balanced and alertly there, a shift happens in consciousness. Rather than being trapped in our usual mind, with its well-formed rut tracks of issues and agendas and ways of thinking, we seem to come from a deeper, steadier, and quieter place. We are present...fully occupying the now in which we find ourselves.

– Cynthia Bourgeault
THE WISDOM WAY OF KNOWING

FOUR
Hearing

Music accompanies us throughout our lives, from our very first
moments to our very last, bringing meaning and heightened
emotional awareness to so many of the important occasions and
experiences that mark our journey on this earth.

– John Bird

THE SPIRITUALITY OF MUSIC

In his book *The Spirituality of Music*, author and musician John Bird gifts us with an up-close and personal look at the healing potential of sound. John tells how his initial spontaneous release of tension and anxiety through a roar-become-chant led him into intentional spiritual practice.

His description of noticing and experimenting with sound vibration in his body puts me in mind of toning, which is practiced in some streams of Buddhism. Toning is the sounding or singing of specific or spontaneous sounds. It is utilized in meditation, prayer, and healing.

I first heard about toning after my aunt Merlin returned from a training intensive in England. Around that time I'd been experiencing persistent and debilitating migraine headaches followed by extended muscle tension pain, so I decided to give toning a try. Comparable to John Bird's experience of release, I found that the extended singing/sounding of a range of notes released a lot of the tension in my body and lessened my pain. Eventually, both the migraines and the attendant muscle tension headaches ceased entirely.

Sound affects us physically and mentally. Music is used for inspiration and healing, particularly as a way to help the brain recover from stroke or injury. Music, especially music with singing, accesses many parts of the brain at once, stimulating connections and improving mental function and capacity. Everything we do that brings the various parts of ourselves (body, mind, and feelings) into communion with each other makes us more fully present to communion with the Holy One and to the joys, challenges, and acts of service that make up the spiritual life.

Hearing/Sound Practice I

Choose a recorded piece of music that touches you in some way, and prepare to hear it repeated three times (see Resources section for more information). Sit comfortably and close your eyes if you wish. Take three or more breaths and "arrive."

The first time the music plays through, hold your focus on the sound and notice if you can feel the vibration of the sound in your body. You may wish to experiment with more or less volume.

On the second and third hearings, allow yourself to hum or sing along if you want. Give yourself permission to sway or dance if your body wants to move.

After three (or more) hearings, turn off the music, sit quietly and rest.

Hearing/Sound Practice II

Choose a time and location where you will be comfortable to make sounds without interruption or self-consciousness. Stand or sit comfortably, and close your eyes.

Breathe consciously for several breaths and arrive.

When you feel present and ready, begin by inhaling and then singing one note for as long as your out-breath lasts. Inhale fully and sing your note again. Sing it as many times as it wants to be sung. You may find that each vocalization stays on one note, or that it rises and falls in pitch, loudness, and speed. Do your best to follow your impulses about what to do next.

Keep making sounds in this way until you notice the sound in your body. Can you feel the vibration of the sounds you're making in your throat or in your resonant chest? In your hands or feet?

As always in life and in spiritual practice, there's no room for self-judgment – either good or bad. There is simply the experience of making sound and feeling it in your body.

When your urge to sound ends, simply stop and stay silent for a time. You may want to be still or you may want to gesture or move in some way.

If you practice centring or contemplative prayer, or any form of mediation, you may wish to follow this sounding with your customary practice.

Sound enters our body through its vibration. It also has the power to stir all manner of emotional memories and to reach and nourish the right side of the brain. Immersing in sound is one of the ways to honour and link our three-mindedness.

Music and musical sounds have great healing capacities.

FIVE.

Seeing

Sacerdos is the Latin word for priest, literally translated as giver of the sacred. Artists, and even their art, can be defined as givers of the sacred. They look at the mundane and the commonplace, and see it as beautiful and meaningful. They watch people dancing and see rhythm and shapes that represent the dance of life. They look at light and shadow, and at the contrasts in life, and see the totality of life. They have painted us angels who traverse the bridge between the worlds. There are countless ways in which artists give us a glimpse of the sacred.

– Jim Kalnin

THE SPIRITUALITY OF ART

As an art-viewer, I like to read or hear at least a little something about each artist or work. I don't like to be told *everything*, because I want the art itself to talk to me, but I find that a few words provide an entry point, an invitation, into the art.

This introduction would not matter so much if we lived in a homogenized society where we all had similar life experience, religion, and world view. But that's not the world we live in. This can be frustrating for the art-maker, who can feel misunderstood or misrepresented. Art-viewers can feel left-out, duped, or just indifferent to the art if there is no common ground. There's so much possible meaning in art today that we can feel quite lost without some written or verbal context.

The tension between word and image is illustrated in the oft-retold anecdote sometimes attributed to Pablo Picasso, and sometimes to Isadora Duncan. When asked to explain their art, he/she responded with something like, *if I could tell you about it, I would not have needed to paint/dance it.*

The simple truth is that visual art is a language other-than, or beyond, words. As such, art often doesn't translate adequately into words. That wouldn't be such a problem except that we tend to dismiss what we can't articulate. But just because we can't articulate an experience doesn't mean it didn't happen. An inability to articulate doesn't mean we haven't been transformed, expanded, or healed in some way.

Taking that idea a step further, Grainger Brown, a gifted psychologist and spiritual director, says that our sleeping dreams do their work even if we don't spend time figuring them out. He says that dreams are of benefit to us even if we don't consciously understand them. The same can be true of the art we see. Not only do we not have to articulate the experience, we don't even have to *get it*. We just need to be open and present.

How many times have we shut ourselves off to seeing a piece of art, or an entire style of art, because we didn't consciously understand it? For that matter, how often have we done that to a person, a whole race of people, or the natural world? This "not shutting off," or presence, is vital training if we want to make peace with our own unknowing. It's learning to live with mystery. Can we recognize in this the parallel to our efforts to articulate spiritual experience? Words and art are woefully inadequate and our attempts to articulate and comprehend the Great Mystery fall short. Images simply offer us another way to experience the sacred, not explain it.

Hear some wisdom from Symmachus, recorded 16 centuries ago: *Not by one avenue alone can we arrive at so great a truth*. Like other forms of art and expression, visual language has the potential to expand our experience of the Holy; it can teach, guide, and encourage us on our journey into ever-deepening relationship with Spirit. Like sound and the breath, visual art can involve our three centres.[1]

Seeing Practice 1

1 Find a piece of art. It can be an original piece that you own or have borrowed, a piece in a gallery, or a picture in a book.

2 The point of this practice is to have your own experience of the art you have selected. Let your reaction/response be whatever it is. Notice what you see. Be aware of moments when you make judgments – positive and negative. Spend meditative and prayerful time looking. Notice things you didn't see at first. Pay attention to anything in the image that feels like an echo of your own life experience, without needing to fully comprehend.

3 The invitation is to trust you, the art, and the Source. There is nothing to *get*, nothing to figure out, and nobody to tell. Just notice. We can build our capacity to trust our own seeing and knowing. We can expand our visual literacy. We can open ourselves to the Holy One in a new way. There are gifts to be claimed in seeing the movement of spirit in new ways.

Seeing Practice II

1 Seek an image that evokes a sense of wonder in you. It might be from your own collection of photos or art, or from an art book or calendar. If an image doesn't present itself, then watch for an object from the natural world. It's best if you can resist the urge to analyze or over-think the selection.

2 For a week or so, spend time with your awe-inspiring image/object every day. If you already have a prayer or meditation practice, you might simply integrate this time of deep-looking into it. If you don't have a standing practice, then choose a

time of day when you are most able to quiet yourself – you'll know your own rhythms best. Let your thirsty eyes drink in wonder during this prayerful time.

3 There are seekers who have spent years contemplating a single icon, object, or painting. Sometimes deep-looking yields surprising epiphanies; sometimes it's a gateway to deep prayer; sometimes an image simply helps us centre ourselves more fully in the present moment – the only moment when we can experience wonder. Whatever happens for you, may these moments of quiet contemplation be a gift in and of themselves.

Seeing Practice III

Some believe that when we get to know each other as people, peace has a chance. As a young art student, I noticed that all the models for life drawing class became beautiful to me as I spent the time to see them well enough to draw them. When we see and hear and know each other it's harder to hold our prejudices. It's harder to hate.

This practice is one of deep-seeing. If you keep Sabbath, you may choose to use some of that time for this deep-seeing practice.

1 Choose a natural object: something living, such as a plant, tree, or cut flower; a rock; a shell; a piece of driftwood; a piece of fruit; or a vegetable. Get a pencil and paper (any type will suffice).

2 Begin by gathering yourself in (centring yourself) by whatever method you use. At minimum, it's helpful to take three mindful breaths to help bring yourself into the present moment.

3 Continue by spending time looking – really looking – at your chosen piece of nature. If your mind tells you that this is a waste of time, and that you already know what a rock looks like (which tends to shut off our seeing), gently replace that thought with an attitude of discovery and keep looking. Look for several minutes.

4 Pick up your pencil and while continuing to look at your chosen piece of nature, slowly and meditatively draw it. Do this without looking at the paper. This is not about drawing; this is about seeing. Something in the process of looking carefully enough to be able to make marks on paper turns our looking into seeing. This is an important distinction in our relationship with all of creation. Its parallel in the verbal realm is the difference between listening and hearing.

Creativity is not a noun or even a verb – it is a place,
a space, a gathering, a union, a where – wherein the
Divine powers of creativity and the human power of
imagination join forces. Where the two come together
is where beauty and grace happen and, indeed, explode.
– Matthew Fox
CREATIVITY: WHERE THE DIVINE
AND THE HUMAN MEET

---

1 Lois Huey-Heck and Jim Kalnin, *The Spirituality of Art*.

SIX

Moving

Our body is ourself. It is our only perceptible reality. It is not
opposed to our intelligence, to our feelings, to our soul. It
includes them and shelters them. By becoming aware of our body
we give ourselves access to our entire being —
for body and spirit, mental and physical, and even strength
and weakness, represent not our duality but our unity.

— Therese Bertherat
The Body Has its Reasons

(It) was a tragic event in the history of western civilization. In the divorce of spirit from flesh, we lost respect for the body and eventually we forgot that is was part of sacredness. ...I believe we each hold a spark of the original light of creation within us. I've seen it light up people's faces and bodies when they dance. In a thousand ways it has been revealed to me that God is the dance and we need only disappear in the dance to liberate the sexual, creative, and sacred aspects of the soul.

– Gabrielle Roth

SWEAT YOUR PRAYERS

In a book that I've long forgotten the title of, I read the words of a First Nations elder who said that Westerners tend to be oblivious to the great wisdom treasures that are our bodies. She said that we treat our bodies like an old rag tied to our consciousness. The truth of the statement pierced me and I've never been quite the same.

Around the same time (about 20 summers ago), I participated in a week-long movements program at Naramata Centre. In our group of about a dozen people was a man who had been head-injured at birth. I'll call him Richard. Richard was able to be part of the group because his aged mom and aunt attended with him. I liked Richard. He had a boyish trusting manner, and he laughed easily.

As the week progressed, we worked sometimes with just one or two others. We were having some powerful experiences in and with our bodies and I was thirsty for the healing and integration that was being poured out. One morn-ing, Theresa asked us to form groups of three. I am embarrassed and ashamed to say that when my little group of three formed and Richard was part of it I felt (secretly, I hope) sad and disappointed. I believed that it would be a care-taking time instead of a "real" experience.

I no longer remember the particular movements, the music, or the process. What I do remember vividly is the moment when the three of us in our little cluster found ourselves in such deep, soulful communion with one another that I began to weep. We were seeing each other; we were being seen by each other; we were all whole people, wholly present for and with each other. It was one of the most real meetings I've ever had with anyone. It was beyond words. Richard was my friend, my equal, and my teacher.

Movement Practice 1
Arriving

When talking about the importance of movement practices, my friend Chris Burns reflected on her experience and understanding that, while our mind tends towards the future and our heart can be drawn to the past, it's our body that's fully in the present. Focusing on breathing is a powerful way to be in the body here and now.

In your own preferred way, focus on your breathing for a few minutes. When you are ready to continue, bring attention and care to your body through one or both of the following practices.

Release

You'll need a tennis ball or equivalent-sized medium-soft ball. Standing in sock-covered or bare feet with your knees soft (slightly bent), roll the ball around under your right foot for five minutes. *(The five-minute silence track on the enclosed CD works well as a timer.)* Visualize the ball massaging every part of the bottom of your foot, including your toes and heel. Apply some pressure, but ease up if you encounter any tender areas. After five minutes, release the ball and stand still for a minute or two. Feel any difference in your feet.

2 Slowly bend forward from your waist, arms hanging forward and fingers reaching towards the floor. Don't go further than your range of comfort. Pause for a moment in this hanging position and notice any differences between the right and left sides of your body. When you are ready, slowly push up from your knees.

3 Repeat (1) with your left foot.

Flow

1 Stand with feet shoulder-width apart and knees soft, arms at your sides. Lift and drop your heels several times to help you remember the support of the good earth beneath you. Then imagine your feet as roots planted into the ocean bottom. Find your balance and rootedness. Imagine your arms, hands, and torso as parts of a long sea plant with branches that are free to float on top of the water. Inhale.

2 Exhale and take one small step forward with your left foot. Find your balance and rootedness once again.

3 As you inhale, gently bend your elbows and allow the backs of your hands to float up comfortably in front of you.

4 On your exhalation gently push your hands out in front of you as if they are being moved out on the waves.

5 On your inhalation slowly bend your elbows, allowing your arms to move back towards your body as if floating on an incoming wave.

6 Repeat this simple movement for a few minutes and give yourself over to the sensation of your arms and hands floating in and out on the waves as you neither direct nor resist the movement.

7 When ready to move on, step back with your left foot as you inhale and repeat the practice with your right foot stepping forward.

My qigong mentor Hajime Naka taught this movement as a way to experience going with the flow. It's important to notice that this is not groundless "drifting off" with every change of current. This sea plant is solidly rooted in the ocean floor where the water is still, while the stem and leaves remain flexible in response to the powerful movement of surface waves.

The practice of knowing our rootedness in the Holy and flowing with the great currents of life is extremely beneficial for soul and spirit. Our body becomes a teacher and mentor to our thinking and emotional centres through the repeated experience of this fluidity.

Movement Practice II
A Body Prayer from the Christian Tradition

I'm not sure where this prayer originated, but I've encountered it in many worship, retreat, and educational settings. The form, words, and gestures vary very little from one leader to another.

1 Centre

Stand comfortably, knees soft. Bring your palms together and let your thumbs lightly touch the centre of your chest. Bow your head and centre yourself.

2 I bow to the earth

Bend forward from the waist, keeping your back straight, and bow to the earth. After a short pause, return to your upright position.

3 I open to the Divine

Bring your arms up above your head, palms facing each other.

4 I include everyone

Draw a large circle in front of you
by bringing your arms out in front
of your chest. Touch the tips of
your middle fingers together lightly.

5 I include myself

Cross your arms, hands on shoulders in a self-hug.

6 I bless it all

Bring your arms out from your body
sideways, a right angle bend at the
elbow, and face your palms forward (a
gesture of surrender). You might turn
your body from side to side to take in
a 180-degree view, or slowly turn a full
circle in your spot.

7 I wake up myself and the world

Clap your hands together vigorously.

8 I bow in gratitude to the earth and to the One

Bend forward from the waist, keeping your back straight, and bow to the earth. After a short pause, return to your upright position.

9 Repeat as often as you wish.

Movement Practice III
A Five Elements Tai Ji

This practice is also adapted from teacher/mentor Hajime Naka, who seeks the essence of the practices over rigid adherence to form.

1 Centre

Stand with soft knees, your feet shoulder width apart, arms at your sides.

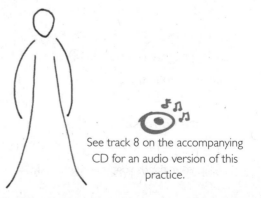

See track 8 on the accompanying CD for an audio version of this practice.

2 Open the gate

Bring your arms up and across
your chest and then open them
wide as you step back with your
left foot. *(I recall my intention to
open all of myself to Life right in
this moment. To be fully here. To be
awake.)*

3 See the mountain

Leave your arms extended and
move them (a quarter turn) so the
right arm is up and the left arm is
down as if holding a huge ball out
in front of you.

4 The five elements

FIRE

Bring your arms down towards the ground and make a
gesture of scooping upwards to waist height saying, "Draw
up earth energy." While making a large gathering motion
with your arms raise your right foot off the ground in front

of you. Place it back on the ground while you make a gesture of pushing forward with your arms, saying words like, "extend fire-energy in life-giving action." Finish this cycle by raising your arms and hands to the sky, saying, "earth-fire gives way to water."

WATER

Slowly bring your arms down, waving your fingers gently to simulate rainfall. Say, "Receive the gift of cleansing, life-giving water – the energy of the heavens." When your hands are down at your sides, stretch your left arm down towards the earth and your right up towards the sky and then bring them together in a gathering motion in front of your waist, saying, "The life-giving energies of earth and heaven co-mingle and nourish the roots of woodwind."

WOODWIND

Turn your right foot and body one-quarter turn to the right while extending your arms and hands straight out in front of you. Start to turn *slowly* back to your forward starting position and continue around (more than 360 degrees) to return to your first starting place. As you turn, say, "Woodwind. Every thing I've ever seen, everywhere I've ever been, everyone I've ever known, every decision, every choice, everything. It has taken *everything* that has happened to bring me to this moment right now. If this mo-ment right now, as I breathe and move, is a good moment, then what could be wrong with any of what has transpired in my life up to now?"

AIR

Rest in a comfortable standing posi-tion, saying, "Here I stand rooted to the earth, held in the embrace of sky. I open to the wind of the Spirit blow-ing through me, releasing my attach-ment to past and future." Visualize yourself as a healthy tree – strong-yet-flexible – and let your trunk and branches dance in the wind.

METAL

Stand again where you started and make a wide gesturing motion with your left arm and then your right. Cup your hands nearly together in front of you as if you're holding a ball. "Metal. I gather up all my gold, I gather up all my earthly treasures and drop them into the water like a rock." Gesture the dropping of the "ball" you were holding. "The water level rises (raise arms, palms up, to shoulder level) and sinks back into the earth" (with palms down, arms return to rest by your sides).

5 Integration

- With your arms at your sides, stretch your fingertips towards the ground. Turn your palms up and *gather earth essence* as you slowly raise your hands and *touch the sky* by stretching your arms upwards as high as your level of comfort allows.
- *Embrace life force* by drawing your two hands together over the middle of your chest, and "return to centre" moving your hands downwards and out to the side, palms face down.
- Raise your left arm up and out in front of you forming a C shape with your hand and say, "The crescent of the Yin moon – my *being*." Then raise your right arm in the same way and form a ball with your hand, saying, "And the orb of the Yang sun – my *doing*."

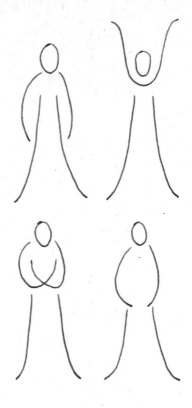

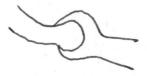

Bring the orb inside the crescent, saying, "In dynamic union."

○ Draw your joined hands in towards your chest and bow deeply from your waist, giving thanks to the Great Unity.

Movement Practice IV
Dancing Presence

Grace is not dependent on stature, flexibility, intelligence, or training. It is just there, accessible in every moment. The key is to listen to what your body wants.

– Cynthia Winton-Henry
WHAT THE BODY WANTS

I live in a small oasis of big, old, indigenous evergreen trees – ponderosa pine and Douglas fir. Strong winds roaring off the nearby lake exert a lot of force on these grandparent and great-grandparent trees. Mostly the trees have enough flexibility to give and move with the currents, and in our time here only a couple of trees have suffered significant damage. In one case, part of the double top of a fir fell right alongside the house; another time a huge gnarled upper limb from the 100-year-old ponderosa crashed down.

When big winds howl through here, I pray for the trees in the neighbourhood. I pray that they will keep dancing, because that's how they'll stay whole. When they lose their flexibility – when they dry or harden – they are at risk of breaking. I'm like that too.

For many years, movement has been part of my morning spiritual practice. Although durations and particular forms ebb and flow, the practice of connecting to the Divine through movement is constant. And most often I connect through mindful dance. And yes; dancing – or any kind of attending to the body in fact – can raise our "stuff."

Gabrielle Roth's well-articulated and well-supported template has been a great companion in my dance practice. As she says, "The *5Rhythms* is a practice both poetic and practical, fluid and focused, a marriage of art and healing that directly addresses the divorce of body from heart, heart from mind that has so plagued our cultures." Amen and Blessed Be.

Roth's five universal rhythms in music and life are

- Flowing (smooth, continuous, grounded)
- Staccato (angular, stop-and-start, fiery)
- Chaos (everything goes)
- Lyrical (playful, sensuous, transformative)
- Stillness (gentle movement with pregnant pauses, integrative)

The practice is to hold the essence of these rhythms in consciousness while expressing them through free-form dance. It is also to live into these universal energies (the energies of life) in order to expand our repertoire of responses to life, be more fully ourselves, and be open and flexible enough to dance with the movement of the Spirit as it blows in and around and through us.

When I started my personal mindful dance practice, I found it extremely helpful to use some of the music Roth has recorded with *The Mirrors*. From time to time I return to that music and to Roth's DVDs as a refresher. I use music from my own collection as well. This allows me to customize my practice session with music that best suits the state of my soul on any given day. But — and I can't say this too strongly — the most important thing is to try this. Don't wait until you have the perfect music or you've learned everything there is to learn. Like all practice, this is a dynamic thing, and we learn by doing.

You can start with just one piece of music that stirs you and move to that. If you don't know where to start, breathe and be still until some part of you is ready to move. It might be one hand, or even one little finger. Just let it begin and then allow your whole body to follow. By moving to a piece of music, we can move our stuck-ness, open ourselves, and become present.

With time, you'll be able to identify the five rhythms in most of your music. There are some days when I need to stay with just one rhythm for my whole session. Sometimes I only need to be "in the flow," and sometimes I need just stillness. Other days, I need to celebrate and express and practice moving in all-out chaos.

Your body is wise. As you practice following its guidance, your own practice of "dancing presence" can unfold.

See the Resources section for more on Gabrielle Roth.

Movement Practice ✓
Walking Meditation

In any consideration of moving practices, walking meditation needs honourable mention. Another practice that's all the better for its utter simplicity, walking meditation basically involves walking slowly with the kind of mindful presence you've already been cultivating. If you are interested in more information, Thich Nhat Hahn has written a practical and inspiring book fittingly called *Walking Meditation*.

God has stamped a rhythm in human beings, animals, plants and even stones. A person walking, a bird flying, a leaf falling — everything proclaims the beginning of a dance. At the heart of the atom, in the ballet of the stars, rhythm and harmony have been sown by our Creator!...Music... dance — these are true prayers.
— Cynthia Winton-Henry
WHAT THE BODY WANTS

SEVEN

Stillpoint

Nothing in all creation is so like God as silence.
— Meister Eckhart

When we sit in stillness we are profoundly active.
Keeping silent, we can hear the roar of existence.
Through our willingness to be the one we are,
We become one with everything.
— Gunilla Norris
INVITING SILENCE

The stillness...awaits a soul to breathe in the mystery that all things exhale in their craving for communion...Our awareness of God is a syntax of the silence in which our souls mingle with the divine, in which the ineffable in us communes with the ineffable beyond us. It is the afterglow of years in which soul and sky are silent together, the outgrowth of certainty of the abundant, never-ebbing presence of the divine.

– Abraham Joshua Heschel

...sit down, take a deep breath and return to the silence and stillness at the heart of the world. Even the ordinary rhythm of day and night has something to say to us. It speaks in silence...

– Kathleen Norris

INTRODUCTION TO MUSIC OF SILENCE

Be still and know that I am God.

– Psalm 46:10

*A*cross traditions, cultures, and time, stillness has been valued as a way to restore our connection with Spirit, our deepest selves, and all of creation. The rich variety of ways to experience the "stillpoint" attests to the value of suspending our busy "doing." The inestimable number of people who intentionally practice stillness is ample testament to its life-giving potential.

It's the simplest thing, it's the hardest thing. The basic instruction makes it seem pretty easy: be still. But choosing to do no-thing remains profoundly counter to popular culture with its attendant pressure to do more, have more, and be more. The concept and forms of stillness are easy to grasp, but encouragement and support for the practice of doing no-thing is harder to come by.

While it may seem that our era has particular challenges, people have struggled for millennia with the compulsion to work, do, and consume. Hence the need for the practice of keeping Sabbath – not only once a week but also in small daily Sabbath-moments and in extended Sabbath retreats in the rhythm of the year.

There are many variations on the practice of stillness. The range of choices means there's a practice for every seeker. It can also become a reason and an excuse for not getting started.

Very simply stated, there are two kinds of silence – intentional and free.

INTENTIONAL SILENCE

Within the genre of intentional silence, there are three primary methods of practice: awareness, concentrative, and surrender.

Awareness practice involves the development of an inner witness or witnessing presence that observes the information that comes to consciousness and also sees consciousness itself. For example, the Buddhist awareness practice of vipassana uses concentration to observe the body, its sensations, or insight that arises.

Concentrative practice features single-point attention to something such as a mantra, the breath, the Jesus Prayer, or an image. For example, Christian meditation uses a sacred phrase (sometimes called a mantra).

Surrender practice requires letting go or releasing the thoughts that arise during the time of meditation. When the mind

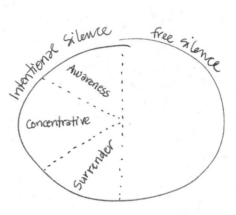

wanders, thoughts are surrendered by the silent saying of a simple pre-chosen word that's not too emotionally charged. Centring prayer is a surrender practice.

All intentional silence (meditation) is intended to still the frenetic activity of what is aptly named the monkey-mind. All forms of meditation are forms of prayer. As Cynthia Bourgeault says, "Prayer is listening to God's silent wordless communion of being."

FREE SILENCE

Within each of us there is a silence – a silence as vast as the universe. We are afraid of it…we long for it. When we experience that silence, we remember who we are: creatures of the stars, created from the birth of the galaxies, created from the cooling of this planet, created from dust and gas, created from the elements, created from time and space…created from silence.
— Gunilla Norris
INVITING SILENCE

Silence reveals. Silence heals. Silence is where God dwells. We yearn to be there.
— Gunilla Norris
INVITING SILENCE

Free silence has neither the development of a witness, nor the concentrative focus of Christian meditation, nor the surrender focus of centring prayer. What free silence offers is the potential for another kind of communion – one that can be the source of specific kinds of redemption, healing, and insight.

There are things we can do to remove obstacles to the experience of free silence, such as making space and time, setting our intention, and being receptive. Even so, the depth experience that is possible in free silence – the direct experience of Unity (that is, mystical experience) – is ultimately a matter of grace. Mystical experience cannot be planned, manufactured, or anticipated with certainty. The best we can do is slow down and be open.

A PRACTICE THAT CALLS US

Whichever path brings us to practice, at the centre there is silence –
perennial, universal, inclusive, radiant. Our true peace and home.
– Gunilla Norris
INVITING SILENCE

While many people devote themselves to deepening into one practice, others find it life-giving to develop a repertoire of practices to draw on. For others yet, one practice is absolutely right for several years until another form calls them.

The following practices offer the opportunity to experience entering three kinds of silence.

Stillness Practice 1
Chant & Concentrative Silence

It helps to decide how much time we will sit each day. Such a boundary around the vastness of
silence makes it less difficult. It's good to start small. Five minutes. Ten minutes. Do-able minutes.
– Gunilla Norris
INVITING SILENCE

When chant music stops, sometimes quite abruptly, an audible silence reverberates throughout the room…This silence is not merely sound's absence, but a mysterious presence, the immense nothingness that is our origin and our home. If we listen carefully, we discover that when all is said and done, chant inducts us into this silence that is the ground of our being.

– David Steindl-Rast
Music of Silence

Cynthia Bourgeault would concur with Steindl-Rast; she teaches that there's a profound connection between chant and intentional silence. It's as if the wash of sound and vibration in chant clears the way for us to release all sound so we can rest in the quiet. Indeed, there's something very powerful about immersing in sound and vibration and then entering silence.

This practice invites you to follow your immersion in sound with a period of concentrative silence in the tradition of Christian meditation.

Preparing

1 Choose a phrase to repeat to yourself during the stillness following the chant. Here are some possibilities:

- Love is all
- Be still and know that I am God
- I am in the web of life
- Silence is a friend that claims me
- I am here

2 Choose a chant to sing for five minutes. It may be one you already know and can sing on your own. It may be one you have recorded that you can sing along with. If your recorded chant is not repeated for five minutes or longer, set your player on repeat so it will automatically replay the chant until you're ready to stop.

You might also use tracks 9 (five minutes of chant) and 7 (ten minutes of silence) from the accompanying CD. The words of the chant are

If you're not using the silence track on the CD, you'll need to decide in advance how long you wish to sit and either set a timer or have a clock nearby that you can check without overly interrupting your stillness.

Be still and know that I am God
Be still and know that I am
Be still and know
Be still
Be

The Entryway

1 Breathe deeply several times while visualizing your breath going right down into your belly. Expand your abdomen outwards on the inhalation to make space for the breath. On the exhalation, release the breath with an audible sigh.

2 Begin to sing the chant. Sing it many times. Sing until you are comfortable with the words and melody; sing until you don't have to think about it anymore; sing until your voice seems to start in your abdomen. Sing until you feel the physi-

cal vibration of your voice in your torso. Sing until you aren't watching yourself anymore. Sing until you are *just singing*. Sing until the chant is moving through you as if you are being sung.

3 When you are finished singing, sit comfortably and rest your hands in your lap, with palms upright and fingertips gently touching. Thich Nhat Hahn suggests having a light smile on your face. Begin to repeat your chosen phrase to yourself slowly and reverently. When you notice that your mind has wandered, gently come back to your phrase. Resist any urge to change your phrase partway through the silence. Let your phrase be the container for this time of silent communion with the Holy.

4 Stand and stretch, and end with a word or gesture of gratitude.

Stillness Practice II
Movement & Sitting-Surrender

You have to dance through the dark in order to see the light. You have to go to the source of all wounds, the big wound, the divorce of spirit from flesh, and heal this wound if you ever want to fulfill the longing for a real self, a soulful self, a big, huge self, one that sleeps with the Beloved. I want to take you to a place…of pure light that holds the dark within it. It's a place of pure rhythm that holds the stillpoint. It's a place within you.

– Gabrielle Roth
SWEAT YOUR PRAYERS

When you meditate, don't soar too high. Don't worry about distractions; they are the stuff of your soul and tell you who you are. Don't try to be good or perfect. Just be.

— Thomas Moore

What Cynthia Bourgeault says about the symbiotic relationship between chant and silence also rings true in the relationship between moving and sitting. Gabrielle Roth says, "The whole object of meditation is to still the mind. The fastest way to do that is to move the body." It's true for me — I can't really "sit" until I engage my body and am consciously in it.

The following is an invitation to experience an embodied entry into a surrender practice known as centring prayer.

Preparing

1 Choose a movement practice from Chapter six. It can be anything that appeals to you today.

2 Choose a humble little word to act as a reminder to surrender all thoughts (even prayers for others and great altruistic plans) for the duration of your sit. Some possible words include *open, quiet, stillness, stillpoint, present,* and *peaceful.* This word is not a magic word. It is simply shorthand for, "I choose to surrender my thoughts in this moment."

The use of a surrender word works because repeating such a long intention can be a distraction in itself. A word that is too evocative or too numinous can also distract, so avoid words that are charged.

If you're not using one of the silence recordings on the CD (track 4, 7, or 10), you'll need to decide in advance how long you wish to sit for and either set a timer or have a clock nearby that you can check without overly interrupting your stillness.

The Entryway

1   Give your body a stretch by raising your arms as high as they will comfortably go. Stand up on your toes if you can. Then let your body slowly fall forward, letting your arms fall towards the floor as far as they can comfortably go. Know your limit, stretch within it. Slowly return to standing upright and give your body a little wiggle to loosen it up. Notice any places of discomfort or tightness that may need care as you move.

2   Do three to five minutes (or more) of movement from the practice you have chosen.

3   When you have finished moving, sit comfortably with your hands resting in your lap, palms upright and fingertips gently touching. Thich Nhat Hahn suggests having a light smile on your face. It can be helpful to restate your intention with a prayer such as, "I choose to surrender all thoughts for the sake of deepening into Spirit." Recall your humble little word and say it to yourself with your first few inhalations.

Each time you notice that your thoughts have wandered (as thoughts will), repeat your surrender word to yourself.

4 End with a word or gesture of gratitude.

Please remember that the point of this meditation is not to achieve perfection, but rather to practice surrendering into the One. Father Thomas Keating recounts a story of a nun who came to him distressed over her failure at centring prayer. She basically told Fr. Keating that she was absolutely hopeless – that in a 20-minute sit her mind wandered a thousand times. The wise teacher reportedly replied,

"How wonderful – a thousand opportunities to practice surrender."

Cynthia Bourgeault also highly values this practice of sitting surrender and reminds us that a sit with few distractions and longer silence is great, and a sit with many distractions and only moments of silence is also great. There's no way to waste time in this practice.

Stillness Practice III
Sensation & Free Silence

Enter into the Silence, into the
Heart of truth;
For herein lies the Great Mystery
Where life is ever unfolding;
Herein the Divine Plan is made known,
the Plan all are invited to serve.

Listen for the music of the Holy Word
in the resounding Silence of
the universe.
– Nan Merrill
PRAYING THE PSALMS

At first silence feels like a place you go to but it becomes a place you come from.
– Cynthia Bourgeault

This practice works very well in the context of a personal/silent retreat.

Preparing

Create a space of an hour or so where you won't be interrupted. Have your journal, note pad, or sketchbook at hand. You might wish to have one of the silence tracks (track 4, 7, or 10) from the accompanying CD ready.

The Entryway

Take a few mindful breaths (*I know I am breathing in, I know I am breathing out…*).

As a way of checking in with your physical self, scan your body for sensation, such as tension, pain, congestion, tingling, numbness, or a stir-of-energy. As Gunilla Norris says, "noticing the particulars we can also begin to notice the space in which they are held…the vastness that holds everything – the great lap of silence."

2 Give your full attention to the part of your body where you are feeling sensation (or each part in turn if there is more than one). Feel whatever is going on. Be discerning about whether something needs to be done, such as visualizing your breath coming into the area, touching the spot, or moving in some way. Check in with that part of you to see if there's anything it wants you to know.

3 Ask yourself if there's anything else the body wants before you move to the next step.

4 Write whatever comes to mind in your journal. It may be in response to your breath, to what you felt and observed in your body, or something completely "other." Write your stream-of-consciousness (whatever comes up) without censor. In her classic book *The Artist's Way*, Julia Cameron promotes the benefit of writing three pages every day. Write three or more pages. Write until you are finished.

5 Sit comfortably with your eyes closed. Return your attention to your breathing and be centred in your body in present time.

6 Settle into the silence with no agenda other than to be present. If you find yourself making to-do lists, bring yourself back to the present moment and your intention to drop into silence. Be as present as possible to whatever emerges. Follow impulses that serve your purpose of deepening communion with God.

7 When the time of silence is done, return to your journal and write/draw in response to or in gratitude for whatever came to you in your time of free silence.

Wise are those who learn through
           silence;
      learn then to listen well.
For beyond the silence and stillness
           within,
      you will come to know a profound and dazzling Silence.
Herein lies the music of the spheres,
      the harmony of creation.
Enter into the holy temple of your soul,
      converse with the Beloved in
           sweet communion.

— Nan Merrill
PRAYING THE PSALMS

Eternity is not a long, long time. Eternity is the
opposite of time: It is no time. It is, as Augustine
said, "The now that does not pass away."
      ...it is accessible at any moment as
      the mysterious fullness of time.

— David Steindl-Rast
MUSIC OF SILENCE

EIGHT

Divinas

(LECTIO & IMAGEO)

An ancient form of meditation on scripture where one reads
"very slowly through a text until a word or phrase 'lights up' and
attracts the reader..."
– Martin Smith

Lectio Divina is Latin for divine reading, spiritual reading, or "holy
reading," and represents a traditional Christian practice of prayer
and scriptural reading intended to promote communion with God...
– wikipedia.org/wiki/Lectio Divina

The practice begins with a slow, out-loud reading of the passage (lectio), allowing it to resonate in the body and engage the moving centre. The next stage, called meditatio, engages the intellectual centre. The (hearer) may visualize, ponder the meaning of the words, allow nuances to suggest themselves...At some point this intellectual work gives way to oratio, or prayer, in which the emotional center begins to resonate...the next step (contemplatio)...melds them all together...

– Cynthia Bourgeault

THE WISDOM WAY OF KNOWING

ectio is an ancient practice that comes to us through the Benedictine tradition. The idea and practice of repeated hearing or extended seeing followed by reflection, response, and resting is simple, yet the experience is often engaging, insight-producing, and deepening.

There are four basic "moments" in a *divina* practice. Beyond the standard Latin terms, various words are used to describe the phases and the characteristics of each phase. The following description is an attempt to distill each moment into the essential states of being and doing.

1 RECEIVE

This is the time to drink in a chosen text (*lectio divina*) or a selected image (*imageo divina*). The "work" is to open and receive through your body and senses.

2 NOTICE

Traditionally called *meditatio* or meditation, this phase engages the intellectual centre by providing food for thought. In the East, it might be said that this is an especially good time to remain curious.

3 RESPOND

In the *oratio* (prayer) phase we may respond with silent prayer, spoken prayer, written prayer, painted prayer, gestural prayer, dancing prayer…We offer something back to our encounter with the Spirit – some creative expression from our emotional centre.

4 REST

In the words of Father Luke Dysinger, "Wordless, quiet rest in the presence of the One who loves us has a name in the Christian tradition – *contemplatio*, contemplation."

The following *lectio divina* practice is the traditional divina practice using text. I have also included a newer *divina* using image. Spiritual director Don Grayston also uses dreams as the "text" for a *divina* process. See the Resources section for more information on the *divina* practices.

Lectio Divina Practice

Prepare

Select a text for the day. To get you started, there are suggested texts in the Resources section of the book. Some are also read aloud on track 6 on the accompanying CD. The practice works best if the text isn't too long, as much of the benefit comes from the repeated hearing of the same text.

It's very important to read the text slowly and aloud. If you're with a group, hear the text in a variety of voices. If you are alone, you might read aloud, use one of the recorded texts from the CD, use recorded poetry (such as Coleman Barks reading Rumi), or pre-record yourself reading so you can focus on listening.

Arrive

Bring yourself into silence through attentiveness to your breath (see Chapters one and two). Enjoy the silence for a few moments and set your intention to open yourself to the Holy.

1 Receive

During the *lectio* phase, hear the text about three times. Listen for a word or phrase that seems written in bold or highlighted. After three readings, note that word or phrase in some way. If you're alone you might jot it down; if you're with another/others you might share the word or phrase aloud (without comment or discussion).

Hear the text another three times, this time listening until a word or phrase lights up with a sense of invitation or call.

2 Notice

Meditatio is an invitation to take some time with the word or phrase that has called you. Main- taining an attitude of wonder, you might repeat it quietly to yourself for a while. Give your thinking self some time to ponder its meaning, all the time staying open to some fresh insight/illumination. You may find challenge, comfort, affirmation, clarity, guidance, a sense of peace… Practice suspending all judgment.

3 Respond

Known as *oratio*, the prayer phase is an opportunity to converse with the Holy. Your prayer/response can take many forms. You may wish to sit in silent communion with inner speaking and/or dialogue, or write a prayer in your journal or notebook. Your prayer may also take form in paint or charcoal, or in sound or movement (see *Prayer Response* section below). As in any relationship, our emotional intelligence provides the wisdom to know when to speak and when to listen, the capacity to feel one's own feelings and honour the feelings of the other, and the ability to be fully and truly ourselves (God can handle it).

4 Rest

The quiet receptive state of contemplation is somewhere in between active and passive, and requires focused attention. From and through *contemplatio* one lets go of effort and rests in the Beloved.

Imageo Divina Practice

Prepare

Find a piece of art – an original piece that you have or borrow, a piece in a gallery, or an image in a book. Resist the temptation to over-think your selection. There is no wrong choice in this practice.

Arrive

Bring yourself into silence through attentiveness to your breath (see Chapters one and two). Enjoy the silence for a few moments and set your intention to open yourself to the Holy.

Receive

Seeing/Observing (*Imageo*)

Bring your attention to the image you've chosen and look at it slowly, gently. Savour each aspect of the image and watch for anything that draws your attention. It may be a certain shade of a colour, a shape or line, or it may be a recognizable image or symbol. This can be very subtle so do not be discouraged if the looking does not bring huge epiphanies.

This is an opportunity to be in the presence of the Holy, to seek the Holy in stillness. The invitation is to move ever more deeply into awareness of Spirit by remaining attentive and present to the image in front of you. There is no other agenda than simply to see. When your mind wanders, gently bring your focus back to the image and remember your intention to see what is right in front of you.

2 Notice
Meditation (*Meditatio*)

Allow the image to enter you. Notice everything in the image and in your reaction to it. If you have no feeling response whatsoever, notice that. Trace the lines/shapes/forms with your eyes (and your fingers if possible/if you wish). You may imagine something of the story behind the picture.

Commit the image to memory by looking deeply and letting it into your inner being. This may bring up all manner of associations. Accept them all and trust that what surfaces during this time is meant to be brought to your consciousness and into your relationship with Spirit. There is nothing to "get" or figure out from this practice.

One gift of this time is the time itself; another is the gift of deep observation of the image and your own reactions and responses. Accept anything and everything that comes, even the "negatives" of boredom, impatience, or judgment. Stay with your inner memories, thoughts, and feelings; bring your whole self into awareness of Presence. Know that visual language can be the language of the Holy One. Let it offer you sustenance for the day.

3 Respond
Prayer (*Oratio*)

Offer to the Holy One what you have discovered in yourself through seeing and meditating. As with *lectio divina*, your prayer/response can take many forms: from sitting in a sense of silent communion, to inner speaking and/or dialogue, to writing a prayer in your journal or notebook. Prayer may also take form in paint or charcoal, sound or movement (see *Prayer Response* section below). Respond as freely as you would to one who knows and loves you. Experience yourself as the holy one that you are. In this consecration-prayer our real selves may be touched and transformed by our awareness of the Divine Presence, no matter how fleeting or how certain.

4 Rest
Contemplation (*Contemplatio*)

End this time by consciously resting in loving Presence. Sink into awareness and acceptance of whatever is happening in you, and hold it all gently. As we began, so we enter into silence once again. Fr. Luke Dysinger reminds us, "*No one who has ever been in love needs to be reminded that there are moments in loving relationships when words are unnecessary. It is the same in our relationship with God. Wordless, quiet rest in the presence of the One who loves us has a name in the Christian tradition —* contemplatio, *contemplation.*"

After the word has been ingested by the body, tasted by the cognitive mind, and digested by the feeling self comes a time when your three minds may "come together" in a restful silence, and the nutrients of your experience may be assimilated. While this is not an active state, it is not exactly passive. It's somewhere between – a receptive place that requires focused attention.

From and through *contemplatio* one may surrender all effort and sink into the Great Love. Much of the teaching of the mystical and wisdom traditions moves us towards the act of conscious, healthy surrender. Marion Woodman says that we need to tend our egos in order to make them secure, strong, and flexible enough to be able to surrender fully and willingly into service of the Divine. Amen.

Prayer Response

Whether you begin with a text (as in *lectio divina*) or with an image (as in *imageo divina*) your prayer response can take many forms. You might stay with words (thought, spoken, or written) or with silence. You might also pray with sound, movement, or visuals.

O Praying with Sound

You can use one of the sound practices from Chapter four; sing or chant something you already know; start with a sound and follow it, improvising your sounds as you go; or you can sing the following very simple chant. All words are sung on the same note. Just find a note you like and stay with it. (This piece is found on track 9 on the accompanying CD.)

Be still and know that I am God

Be still and know that I am

Be still and know

Be still

Be

(Repeat until done.)

○ **Praying with Movement**

The embodied prayer practice from page 52 can work as a prayer response to either lectio or imageo divina. Let your prayer gestures and movements flow from the awareness you are holding from the receive and notice phases. If nothing seems to want to flow, be still, breathe deeply, and watch for any urge to move, no matter how subtle it may be. It might just be to move only your baby finger or one of your feet. Wherever there's an impulse or even a willingness to move, let the movement begin and let that part of your body lead the rest of you into prayerful movement. This can seem strange at first because many of us are unaccustomed to thinking of our bodies as having the capacity to pray, but sometimes it's exactly our un-ease that opens a window to the Holy.

○ **Praying with Visuals**
If you don't have any art supplies

Gather some paper (most anything will do) and something to draw or paint with. It's recommended that you choose something like crayons, pastels, or charcoal – something that doesn't let you get too fussy about the results – but use what you have. It's better to use a fine-point mechanical pencil or ballpoint pen than to avoid trying this!

When it comes to the prayer time of your practice, put your drawing material in your non-dominant hand (right hand if you're left-handed and vice versa) and draw. As in the movement prayer, if you have no idea how to begin, take a few deep breaths and gently hold awareness of what has stirred for you in the first phases.

Sometimes you have a clear sense of what to do (such as "make circular strokes," or "draw a sun, moon, and stars"). Sometimes you just sit until you can start. Wander around the page and see what comes.

It's important to remember that this practice is not about making art. It's about opening yourself to the Beloved in a new way, and allowing your prayer to take the form of line and shape.

For those with some basic art supplies
Have your journal, sketchbook or drawing paper to hand. Collect a piece of clear or white wax (a stub of a white taper candle, a piece of paraffin or a white crayon work just fine), a not-too-small brush (I like the Chinese bamboo brushes), and some water-based media such as a tempera, gouache, or a water-colour set. Chinese or India inks are also well-suited to this practice. Also have a container of water and a cloth or paper towel at hand.

Start your visual prayer with wax on paper, being sure to press quite hard with the wax. The gift of the wax is that it's very hard to see and very hard to control, so it opens an unknown dimension and surrender – both of benefit to our spiritual practices. If you don't have a sense of how to begin, pause, breathe, and wait for an impulse to come through your hand. It's preferable to use your non-dominant hand.

When you're finished drawing with the wax load, "check in" about what colour to start with. You might wet your paper first with water, or begin directly with your chosen colour. Paint prayerfully, paying attention to the impulses about colour choice and where to make the next stroke. One prayer may take more than one piece of paper. Keep going until you are done.

An Informal *lectio Divina*
The Divine Lover

Read and re-read *The Song of Songs* from the Bible.

Start by reading the whole book – it's only eight short chapters. Read it in more than one translation if possible. Read it without commen-

taries. Read with your curiosity fully engaged.

Start to note the words/phrases/ passages that draw your atten- tion. What inspires and attracts you? What, if anything, troubles or repulses you? Focus on those passages and commit to reading them prayerfully – perhaps every day for a week (or longer), or every Sabbath day for a month (or a lifetime).

Watch particularly for places of connection (comfort) and disconnection (unease) with the erotic union that's celebrated in this book of the Bible. You may read *The Song of Songs* as metaphor for our relationship with God. You may read it as an erotic love story that celebrates the sexuality that gives us life and animates our living. Either way, it's a canonical text that contributes a unique understanding of the Holy.

What does this erotic text have to reveal to you about the nature of God? Can you accept "lover" as a face of God? And if yes, how might that change how you live in your body, in relationship, and within the web of creation?

A *divina* approach (that is, prayerful, meditative and receptive attention) can be brought to more than just Holy or inspiring text or an evocative image. Don Grayston practices *divina* as a way to engage with the rich world of dreams. "Praying our dreams" expands our dream-discovery from our thinking centres into our emotional and kinesthetic centres. You may write your dream down and then read it in the first *divina* phase (receive), or you may just bring it to memory and retell it yourself (speaking it out loud is always best if possible). Follow this with the usual phases of "notice," "respond," and "rest." A *divina* approach to our rich, often confusing, and usually puzzling dream world is a powerful way to explore and honour the wisdom that dreams can offer.

NINE

Compassion

A religious (person) is a person who holds God and human
in one thought...who suffers harm done to others,
whose greatest passion is compassion, whose greatest
strength is love and defiance of despair.
— Abraham Joshua Heschel

Compassion is the radicalism of our time.
— Tenzin Gyatso, 14th Dalai Lama

Compassion literally means to feel with, to suffer with. Everyone is
capable of compassion, and yet everyone tends to avoid it because
it's uncomfortable. And the avoidance produces psychic numbing —
resistance to experiencing our pain for the world and other beings.
— Joanna Macy

The act of compassion begins with full attention, just as rapport does. You have to really see the person. If you see the person, then naturally, empathy arises. If you tune in to the other person, you feel with them. If empathy arises, and if that person is in dire need, then empathic concern can come. You want to help them, and then that begins a compassionate act. So I'd say that compassion begins with attention.

— Daniel Goleman

The opening quotes make it abundantly clear that while living compassionately is a noble calling, it isn't exactly easy. Facing human suffering seems to be getting harder as news quickly travels throughout our global village and we hear plenty of horrendous stories. We can get overwhelmed with so much bad news coming at us daily.

It's because compassion is uncomfortable (even painful at times) that Joanna Macy says "everyone tends to avoid it." But the cost of avoiding it is high – not only for those deprived of our compassionate response, but also because a habitual response of avoidance numbs our ability to feel *anything*. As a wise teacher once told me, we can't cut off our feelings selectively; when we avoid feeling pain, our capacity for joy (and every other emotion) is diminished to the same extent. Even though we know all the good reasons for "feeling with" others, we have to accept that our own resistance to compassionate living will arise. Thus, we acknowledge

that ongoing intention, commitment, and practice are needed to sustain it.

When we talk about paying attention to something difficult, we say that we need to "face it." Facing it not only implies that we need to turn our face towards the situation or person; it also suggests that we need to give the situation a human face, or see the human face of suffering. Daniel Goleman says we begin by paying attention and really seeing the other.

Margaret Wheatley writes, "We can turn away or we can turn toward. Those are the only two choices we have." She goes on to describe the practice of bearing witness – turning toward another and allowing their experience into our life. She herself does this by finding an image of a person or persons affected by a current situation of suffering. She then chooses to look carefully and thoroughly so that she is aware of their plight. In the process of deep seeing, she makes a conscious effort to open her heart to their suffering.

Paying attention by putting a face to the people affected by government death squads, Apartheid, native reservations, genocide, rape, human trafficking, or starvation is what we are first called to do. This seeing takes psychological and spiritual maturity and some serious practice. We begin where we are and from there build our capacity for attention and compassion.

Paying attention or bearing witness (*Practice I* below) is a good way to enter the Buddhist practice of tonglen (*Practice II* below). Both are ways of facing the reality of suffering rather than turning away or becoming hard-hearted. Trying to avoid suffering only leads to more suffering. It all puts me in mind of the Borgian mantra from Star Trek: *Resistance is futile*.

It's good to remember that when we pay attention to suffering we not only meet our feelings of empathy or sympathy for other people in tragic circumstance, we also encounter our own fear of suffering, pain, and death. We need to take care of ourselves in a practice such as this. If the timing is not right for you, set this aside for another time.

Compassion Practice 1
Attention

Prepare

Find a picture of someone in pain or in need, or an animal or part of the planet that's suffering. The photo may be from a newspaper or magazine, from the Internet, or from your own collection of photographs.

Arrive

Bring yourself into stillness through attentiveness to your breath (see Chapters one and two). Enjoy the silence for a few moments, and then name your intention, such as, "I choose to open my whole self to the person/situation I'm about to see." Bring an attitude of compassionate non-judgment.

See

Sit comfortably with the image on your lap or on a table in front of you. Begin by looking at the particulars of the image in front of you. Stay very descriptive at first with what you can see in the image. Then bring to conscious memory anything you might know about the person or situation. Notice any questions that might arise in you. Invite wonder as you deepen your seeing.

2 Feel

As you continue looking, take time to check in with yourself about any feelings that may arise. Choose to invite all of your feelings, even such things as estrangement or "nothing." Open yourself to fully feel what's within you without judgment, especially if comments such as, "This is silly!" or, "I hate that I cry so easily" come up. Any time we willingly take the risk to feel our feelings, it's important to be gentle with ourselves. John O'Donohue says we are responsible to be "shelterers of our own souls." In other words, begin extending compassion by offering it to your own tender self.

3 Do

Remaining conscious of your observations and feelings, turn your attention again to your chosen photo. Let all thoughts and feelings be touched by Infinite Love and let that love flow through you towards the person/circumstance represented by the photo.

There's a piece of wisdom my aunt shared with me once: "If it's not love, it's fear." Remembering this has helped me in the wee small hours of the night when I've been worried for someone. I visualize my fear being transformed into love and I choose (by grace) to send love toward the person I'm concerned about instead of sending my anxiety, fear, or pain. This one shift has been transformative.

4 End

Offer your gratitude to Love.

Compassion Practice II
Tonglen

A word about tonglen and one of its contemporary teachers, Pema Chodron.

Pema Chodron is a Buddhist nun, author, and teacher. On her CD *Meditation for Difficult Times: Awakening Compassion through the Practice of Tonglen*, she talks about life-difficulties as opportunities to become fully awake. She says that when the energy of difficulty is not all bound up in me and self, it can be tremendously transformative.

Tonglen practice has the potential of awakening our compassionate heart and developing our sense of kinship with all beings. A tonglen attitude of "turning towards" pain can be very healing.

Chodron suggests that we start our practice of tonglen with something that isn't too much for us – that we be gentle with ourself and go only as far as we are willing. As she says, "opening the heart is opening the heart. Start where you can – it's all training." Go only to the level that's comfortable. Be gentle. Facing suffering is challenging work.

Chodron names the tonglen attitude toward suffering as having three levels of courage.

1 The first stage of courage: Tonglen in-the-moment

This is a practice for any time suffering presents itself. When you think of someone you know who's in difficult times, when you hear tragic news, or when you encounter pain in yourself, try the following:

Choose to notice and name it. "Seeing this suffering, I feel _____ (hopeless, angry, sad, guilty, helpless, lonely, scared, etc.). If you feel nothing, or if you feel resistance, notice and name that, being true to whatever comes up.

Having acknowledged your feeling-response, the vital next step is to remind yourself that you are not alone. Pain can be isolating, so it's important to know that many, many others in the human family are experiencing the same feelings you are. Making this connection begins to shift things.

2 The second stage of courage: Staying in touch with your feelings

Name an intention such as, "May this become a path of awakening-the-heart for all of us." It's an act that fits Heschel's "defiance of despair."

3 The third stage of courage: A dedicated tonglen practice

Tonglen literally means taking and sending, and this begins with the breath. On the in-breath, take in pain – your own, that of others, and that of the world. On the out-breath, send out relief. Pema

Chodron says the in-breath is dark, heavy and hot, while the out-breath is calm, cool, and refreshing.

This third stage is the most radical part of this practice. It is the voluntary "taking on" of all similar suffering to that which you are feeling in order to alleviate the suffering of others. It's a profound act of compassion. It starts with the stated intent, "Since I am feeling ___ anyway, may I feel it fully so that others may be free of it." A small sentence to say, but a huge intention to take on. It may take some time to be ready for this.

Chodron cautions against rushing into this stage. It's important to be honest with yourself about whether the present moment is the time for you to take this on.

Historically, the practice of tonglen was used in communities of people with leprosy.

Today, it is used in hospice situations, especially by people with HIV/AIDS and cancer. To live in the reality of one's own suffering and then willingly take it on for the sake of others is profoundly healing on the spiritual level and in some cases on the physical level. (There is much we don't know about prayer, subtle energy, and the power of intention.)

No matter if you've only done the first step or you've gone through all the levels of courage, come back to the practice of tonglen over the next days. You will be expanding your capacity to face suffering and defy despair, and you will be creating the conditions in yourself and in the world for compassionate action.

How far you go in life depends on your being tender with the young, compassionate with the aged, sympathetic with the striving, and tolerant of the weak and strong. Because someday in life you will have been all of these.

— George Washington Carver

Human beings are a part of the whole called by us universe, a
part limited in time and space. They experience themselves, their
thoughts and feelings as something separated from the rest,
a kind of optical delusion of consciousness. This delusion
is a kind of prison for us, restricting us to our personal
desires and to affection for a few persons nearest to us.
Our task must be to free ourselves from this prison
by widening our circle of compassion to embrace all living
creatures and the whole of nature in its beauty.
— Albert Einstein (slightly abridged)

A good motivation is what is needed: compassion without
dogmatism, without complicated philosophy; just understanding
that others are human brothers and sisters and respecting their
human rights and dignities. That we humans can help
each other is one of our unique human capacities.
— Tenzin Gyatso, 14th Dalai Lama

TEN

Hope & Gratitude

HOPE

Hope is the celestial and spiritual counterpart of terrestrial and natural instincts of biological reproduction...In other words, hope is what moves and directs spiritual evolution in the world.

— Valentin Tomberg

Tomberg calls attention to two aspects of mystical hope. The first is its orientation towards evolution...The world is going somewhere, and that [type of] hope is the means by which it gets there. Second he claims that hope is objective — and thus...public. It does not have to do with our own private agendas...Ultimately hope is divine energy and intelligence moving toward the accomplishment of its purposes: it makes use of us rather than we of it.

— Cynthia Bourgeault

TWO KINDS OF HOPE

It turns out that there are two kinds of hope. These two kinds of hope show up in the stories of the Bible even as they do in life. The most familiar one is hope that is tied to a specific outcome. For example, we hope for happiness for our friends and children and for ourselves, and we hope for a better world.

This kind of hope is not a bad thing. What we dare to hope we may also dare to pray for and even work towards. This kind of hope can get us to the next step. And this kind of hope can sustain us in challenging times.

Then there is this other kind of hope: a hope that is not tied to outcomes. This *other* hope (I'll call it deep hope) is important because if *all* of our hope stays tied to a particular outcome, we are in danger of losing *all* hope when the thing we are hoping for doesn't happen.

And just what is this other hope, this deep hope?

Let's turn to the writing of spiritual teacher Cynthia Bourgeault, who lists four characteristics of this deep hope.

It is not tied to a good outcome, to the future. It lives a life of its own, seemingly without reference to external circumstances and conditions.

It has something to do with presence. We have the immediate experience of being met and held in communion by something intimately near.

It has a quality of time-out-of-time. Our usual sense of the passing of the hours and days is altered. Somehow, time can seem suspended. It imbues the moment we are actually in (rather than some future time) with an unexpected vividness and fullness. It is as if we are transported into a wider field of presence, a direct encounter with Being itself.

This quality of being fully present to the moment we're in is vital, as the hand of God can touch us only in the now.

It bears fruit within us in the sensations of strength, joy, and satisfaction: a certain lightness of being. But mysteriously, rather than deriving these gifts from an external source (such as expectations being met), it seems to produce them from within.

GRATITUDE

If the only prayer we ever said was "Thank-you"
it would be enough.
— Meister Eckhardt

Life is given to us; every moment is given. The only appropriate response therefore is gratefulness. When we wake up to the fact that everything is a gift, it is only natural to be thankful and to look on everything that happens as a chance to respond to the Given Life.
— David Steindl-Rast
MUSIC OF SILENCE

When we greet the new day as a gift, a sense of gratefulness can carry us through the hours that follow. The day is presented to us as something to give away to others hour by hour.
— David Steindl-Rast
MUSIC OF SILENCE

Obviously it can be extremely hard to practice gratitude when we are in the depths of pain or grief. Ironically, it can also be difficult to practice gratitude when life is going well. Somehow when life is hard we tend to blame God, curse life. And when life is easy we are more likely to grow forgetful and believe we've done it all ourselves.

A gratitude practice helps us remain conscious of the bigger reality that surrounds us – a reality larger than the individual events of our lives. We can regain a wider perspective by remembering – with gratitude – the miracle that is life.

Practicing gratitude is not to deny hardship or suffering. It's not to be oblivious of the staggering ways we each and all fall short of actualizing a just and peaceful world. It's definitely not insurance against calamity.

Julian of Norwich's assertion that *all shall be well and all shall be well and all manner of things shall be well* is not naïveté. It is not hope for certain outcomes. It is an abiding hope which is grounded in the reality of the Holy One – that no matter what is happening around us, somehow the Beloved is with us, and therefore at the deepest levels of soul, *all shall be well*.

This kind of hope is in symbiotic relationship with gratitude. They affect and nourish each other. Cynthia Bourgeault writes, "When we enter it (mystical hope) it enters us and fills us with its own life – a quiet strength beyond anything we have ever known."

Being grateful even for a few small things is an act of hope, and holding hope is a critical aspect of spiritual life. This deep and abiding hope in Life and in Love – in spite of all evidence to the contrary – affects not only the quality of our individual lives but has a positive impact that ripples out around us. The practice of experiencing and expressing gratitude helps maintain our perspective, courage, and hope – all things that empower us and sustain our life-giving actions (our work) in the world.

A Gratitude Practice
Opening the Day

1 Prepare

If possible rise before the sun and watch it emerge as the earth turns back towards it. Otherwise be somewhere you can see the morning light – outside if weather and location permit.

Have a journal, sketchbook, or paper, and writing/drawing/painting implements at hand.

2 Awaken

Begin with the body prayer on page 52.

3 Receive the gift of a new day

No matter what the circumstances of your life, today you are here, awake and alive, to see another day. As you inhale, consciously *breathe in* the life force. As you exhale, *breathe out* any residual sleepiness.

Breathe out anything standing in your way of living fully in this moment of a brand new day. Stay with your breath awhile. Immerse yourself in the miracle of a new day. Let it soak into your bones.

4 Express your gratitude to the Author of Life

You might do this through prayer, contemplation, writing, chanting/singing, dancing, or drawing/painting. Offer something back in appreciation of the life you've been given. A silent *thank you* can be enough.

5 Integrate

As you prepare to end this time of intentional gratitude, ask for some guidance on how you might remember to be grateful throughout the day. You may have a touchstone word or image, or perhaps a sensation in your body.

There is actually no end to this practice. We already do it in a multitude of ways (sometimes more intentionally than others). When we take time to really see someone, or listen to someone, or appreciate beauty, it's a form of gratitude. This practice is a reminder to build appreciation for "what is" into our days.

Use your touchstone as a reminder throughout the day.

A Gratitude Practice
for Evening

1 Sit comfortably, take a few mindful breaths, and centre yourself.

2 Reflect on any challenging times, people, situations, or news from the day. Recall anything you regret doing or not doing, and notice the thoughts, feelings, and physical sensations that arise as you recount this experience (or experiences).

3 Breathe in and know it is life itself that enters you. Let this life-breath bring healing, forgiveness, and love to the raw or tender places in you. Exhale and release any residual "negativity" from the day.

4 Reflect on the joys of the day: good news, meaningful conversations and encounters, work well done, blessings received. Notice the thoughts, feelings, and physical sensations that arise as you recount these moments.

5 Breathe in, knowing it is life itself that enters you. Allow this life-breath to inspire your gratitude for everything – challenge and blessing. Breathe out gratitude for the gift of the day, and allow the love, forgiveness, healing, blessing, and grace that you have received pour through you and out into the world and all those around you.

6 Express your gratitude to the Author of Life. You might do this through prayer, contemplation, writing, chanting/singing, dancing, or drawing/painting. Offer something back in appreciation for the life you've been given. A silent *thank you* can be enough.

There Was a Time

There was a time...
I remember I could be lost
In the exquisiteness of a single flower.
Sink into the innocence of its perfection.
Be lost in the moment of it...

There was a time.

Many gardens later,
Having dug and heaved and pulled and wrestled with stubborn
stone and tendentious weed.
Having sown seeds,
planted and watered,
staked and tied.
In despair of hope, have gone
with arsenal of tools and potions
to make my garden grow.

So much time.
So many gardens.

Gaining what, I wonder...
The bumper crop?
Imagined profusions of bloom?
The 'right' arrangement to complement
my life's space?

Couldn't I just remember
that all I ever needed
is just one single blossom,
to show me
...if I but care to look...
the tender face of God?

– Beth Weick

AFTERWORD
Cycles

At my home there are two prayer and meditation paths. Walking either one begins with the intention to be as fully present in-the-moment as possible. That is true for the outdoor path that wends around the edges of our half-acre, and it's true of the indoor route which threads through our eighty-year-old built-onto home. The paths are humble. No one could be faulted for not recognizing them as routes to the Sacred.

The indoor and outdoor paths both follow the four directions and encourage spending time in the east, the south, the west, and the north. Both walks also recognize the directions of up and down, right and left, inner and outer.

At this time when my treasured spiritual practice is changing, the prayer paths give me a way to stay grounded (literally and figuratively) while being open to whatever's emerging. Again and again I return to the path, to the directions, to the core practices (breathing, presence, whole-mindedness, movement, stillness, compassion) that re-mind me that all is holy and that we are all one. My practice now shifts more freely in response to what each moment calls forth, but the commitment to mindfully walk the directions remains a framework, an armature for the Great Work – the art of transformation.

EAST

Morning, beginning, the seed and planting, birth, rebirth, resurrection, spring…

I connect east with new beginnings, the potential for healing, rebirth.

Day begins in the east. We are passengers on the earth as she turns back towards the sun and brings day to these longitudes. Whether I am up before the sun is revealed above the horizon line, after it becomes visible in the eastern sky, or at the magic moment when the first rays appear, I am transformed when I notice the arrival of a new day.

And when I pause and notice, the unbidden response to the remarkable gift of a new day is gratitude. As I remember how awesome it is to be given the gift of yet another day, my gratitude goes out to the Author of Life, which includes all the forces it has taken to make life-as-we-know-it possible.

Here I pray for the lands and peoples of the east. I think of the countries and what I know of the issues that face the people. This kind of remembering helps keep me from paralysis and avoidance (*a void dance*).

From a small book on the Chartres Cathedral I read, *Ancient Pilgrims oriented themselves through understanding the theology behind the architecture of the church… East, where the altar was located, directed one's attention to resurrection and heaven.*[1] I adapt that concept and contemplate birth, rebirth and resurrection. I read heaven as the kin-dom,[2] the kin-dom come here and now, the kin-dom we are to recognize and help make manifest. I recall the slogan of the U.K.'s Christian Aid, "We believe in life before death." Amen.

Many associations with the east come to mind, too many to trace but fragments: the "Fool" or "Seed" card of the tarot; the beginning of the journey; the step off the brink not to death but into the unknown. I think of the Taoist concept of being empty in order that there is room to be filled with something new. A fresh new morning can nurture that kind of receptivity.

I often do qigong or tai ji in the morning facing east.

SOUTH

Afternoon, growing, watering, weeding, tending, blooming, summer, the beginning of maturity…

I turn toward south – the direction of enduring light. At our place, outdoor south is the garden; indoor south is the kitchen. Both are places of feeding and nourishment. Outside, I take a side trip up the short stone path and pick and eat a handful of blackberries. This causes me to reflect on the ways I leave the garden, such as when I am estranged from the soil and the process of growing.

How many ways do I/we long to return to the garden? To the paradise of simplicity, where everyone has all they need. Where soil is reverenced as the miracle it is. I smile at the memory of an old joke. Some scientists confront God and say, "You know, we've got it all figured out now, and anything you can do, we can do. Maybe we can even do it better."

"Oh yes?" comments God.

"Yes," the scientists emphatically reply.

"Well then," says God. "You make a person and I'll make a person, and we'll get together and compare."

The scientists, thinking this is going to be way too easy, say, "You're on."

God nods agreement and stoops to pick up a handful of dirt. One of the scientists bends over to pick up a handful of dirt too, and God says, "Oh, no you don't. You make your own dirt."

Tending the outdoor path and walking it mindfully puts my feet on the ground and opens my eyes to the earth in a deeper way. After 19 years of being here, I love it even more now because I know it more intimately. I am connected to this small piece of land in a fresh way. As with people, how can I not love a place once I know it?

Looking south, I pray for the lands and people of the south. Lay Minister Kathy Snider serves some of the poorest in Guatemala. I recall her saying that the poor of the south pray that we in the north will change our dream. The North American dream is killing them. They understand that until we change our dream we will continue to plunder the earth and kill its people and animals.

South (in a medieval cathedral) corresponded to the New Testament and its messages. I am reminded of Jesus' teachings on poverty and wealth as I reflect on changing my/our dream. I hear the words of a gospel song, *None of us is free when one of us is chained.* Help me, Holy One, to live into the new dream – your dream.

A practice of compassion, bearing witness, or tonglen fits well in the south.

WEST

Evening, ending, ripening, fruit, gleaning, autumn, harvesting the wisdom of life-experience…

Now I step towards the lake in the west. Indoors or out I see it through a thinning screen of indigenous Douglas fir and ponderosa pine, Oregon grape and Saskatoon bushes. Indoors and out this is a secluded spot – a great refuge for the introvert in all of us.

The west is where the earth turns from the bright light of the sun toward the reflected light of the moon. We call it sunset, and it can be a spectacle of ever-shifting light, colour, and cloud forms. West also marks endings, both welcome and unwelcome. Coming to terms with the end (death) of habits, values, and dreams we hold dear requires that we be willing to grieve the losses. If we do not do the grown-up work of grieving, we will never adequately recover and move on.

To move on, to begin somewhere, to do something, takes maturity. From Julia Cameron in *The Artist's Way* via my friend Julie Elliot I learn that our task is to identify and then act on the first *do-able* thing, and keep going from there, acting out of appreciation for the magnificence of life, claiming and nurturing a heritage of hope. Our salvation does not lie in the actions of worldly powers and principalities.

The good news is that we are not alone. We can and do "help each other walk the mile and bear the load."[3] We also have the assurance of spiritual belief and the testimony of the holy ones past and present – the conscious circle of humanity, as Cynthia Bourgeault calls it.

There is no assurance of success. We act for justice for the earth and its people because it is the right thing to do. Our will to act comes from the certainty that love is the only way.

West, where the pilgrims would enter (a medieval cathedral) held reminders of death, judgment, and the end of time. I accept the metaphor of end times. Our collective way of life needs to end so that all may live more fully. We can all stand to grow our capacity to let go and let be.

Often I prefer a silence practice when reflecting on the wisdom of the west.

NORTH

Night, resting, fallow, sustained by last season's harvest, winter, winter-of-life as the season of ageing and sageing…

Some retracing of steps is required before the walk turns north. Outdoors I follow the path marked by a line of earth, pine cones and needles, and walk past bleached bones, rusty metal remnants, and weathered wood. The path turns back and

forward and round the fire pit. Inside, I look out at the same scene from my studio and remember with gratitude our status as visitors on this planet. I know north less well than the other directions.

In a lifetime of three-score and ten, I am almost three-quarters of the way around the circle. I have made peace (more or less) with the cycle of light and shadow, the smaller endings and beginnings, and the delightful-yet-fallible creature that I am, and that we all are. I have experienced more than half a century of outer winters along with some inner winters of the soul and psyche, but I have not yet lived the winter season of life. There were times past of threatening illness when I despaired that I would ever live this long. At those times I told myself I would never resent wrinkles and whitening hair and the long-term affects of gravity on certain body-parts. (Some days I do better with this than others!) I pray that if the winter-season be part of my lifespan, I have the grace to live it thoroughly.

At the service for our dear sister-in-law Elaine Kalnin, her brother read the words, "we are not given control over the length of our life, only over its depth." We all nodded, knowing that Elaine lived her life with exuberance and depth. Facing north I pray for the wisdom to accept whatever comes next with grace, good humour, and an open heart. I pray to live it all as fully as possible. I pray we may all have that capacity to live the joy as much as the sorrow.

Facing north I think of the lands and peoples of the circumpolar region. I pray that they continue to find the strength of their own ways and assert the rights of the land, animals, and people. Our invasion of the north is more recent than our invasions of the south in the Americas, but the shock of colliding cultures has still taken a toll. There are many signs of hope in these people whose traditional lands are in an ecosystem so harsh we can barely imagine it. Holy One, may we be wiser this time, and support the people· as they care for the earth.

North in a medieval cathedral represented time and truth in the Hebrew scriptures. This makes north a good place to offer thanksgiving for the gifts of wisdom and tradition in Judaism, the faith of Jesus, and all the enduring world religions. North is an opportunity to set the intention to understand more deeply.

For indigenous people in the northern hemisphere, winter was traditionally the time for rest, introversion, and introspection. The harvest was in, the land was at rest, people and animals hibernated. The Celts and people of other earth-based spiritualities consider winter a time when the "veils *thin* between the worlds" and we are closer to the ancestors and the spirit world.

I like a divina practice in the north — either text followed by prayer, writing or painting, or beginning with contemplation of a great art piece.

ARRIVING WHERE WE STARTED

Whether I'm doing this walking meditation in the house or outside, the last turn takes me back to where I began. My knowledge that I am nurtured by this place has deepened. After mindfully walking, pausing, looking, and listening, I know the building and the land more fully as a place of sanctuary for us and our guests. By walking and praying for the land and creatures of the directions it is ever clearer to me that I and we-in-the-west live in incredible privilege, and that the right response is to "give it all back." The right response is to offer service from our own wellness, our own wholeness.

Like the practice of mindfully walking the directions, all practices could fall under the heading, "the practice of presence." Presence is the main event. Everything else flows from this starting place. It's where we begin and where we end. I am here. Present to myself, to the Beloved and to all the others.

---

1   Jill Kimberly Hartwell Geoffrion, *Praying the Chartres Labyrinth: A Pilgrim's Guidebook.* The cathedral notes for each of the four directions are from this book.

2   I choose the contemporary renaming to kin-dom rather than kingdom, which speaks of the "power-over" of old hierachies.

3   From the contemporary hymn *We Are Pilgrims (The Servant Song)* by Richard Gillard

BLESSING

I leave you with the gift of the three rakus. They came to the Pacific Jubilee Program[1] through long-time staff member Dawn Kilarski who, during our residencies, leads us daily in the practice of presence. The three rakus can ground, encourage, and inspire. They have the potential to change our perspective from nagging petty concerns to grateful cosmological view.

The rakus can be done in less than a minute and they shift everything…

As you say each raku, bow from the waist with a straight back.

I bow to my own work. *(bow and return slowly)*

I bow to the work of others. *(bow and return slowly)*

I bow to the Great Work. *(bow and return slowly)*

---

1   The Pacific Jubilee Program is one of four Jubilee programs across Canada. For more than two decades these programs have offered spiritual seekers ways to deepen spiritually. www.jubileeassociates.ca

RESOURCES

Chapter 1

This chant was given to me (in the indigenous understanding of gifts from the Spirit) when I was on a personal silent retreat at Naramata Centre in 2004. It is yours to copy, distribute, and use freely. © Lois Huey-Heck 2004.

guitar capo 3

Now

G   G   G   D   G   G   G   D   (D)   Em   Em   © Lois Huey-Heck 2004   D   D   Em

Now is the time Here is the place and this is Ho ly Ground

Chapter 3

Cynthia Bourgeault's book *The Wisdom Way of Knowing* is a good summary of whole-mindedness. The entire book is excellent.

The Enneagram, an in-depth means of insight for spiritual unfolding, teaches the wisdom of nurturing our whole-mindedness. A dynamic tool for self-understanding (same as transformation?) and transformation, the Enneagram combines the insights of modern psychology with the wisdom of ancient spiritual traditions. Learn about the Enneagram and look in a new way at how you relate to yourself, to others, and to the universe. An Internet search for Enneagram teachers will yield contacts by name or location. There are also several good books on the Enneagram. Renee Baron and Elizabeth Wagele, *The Enneagram Made Easy* (New York: HarperCollins, 1994) is a good starter and Sandra Maitri's *The Spiritual Dimension of the Enneagram: Nine Faces of the Soul* is an excellent deepening.

The Gurdjieff movements support the integration of the three centres. The best way to experience the movements fully is with an experienced teacher.

The website www.gurdjieff-internet.com links to Gurdjieff related sites worldwide.

For Gurdjieff movements instructors/organizations see:
- www.gurdjieffmovements.org
- www.gurdjieff-movements.net
- www.gurdjieff-internet.com

Melanie Monsour has composed and recorded music to accompany Gurdjieff-type exercises that are related to the nine Enneagram types. She has also recorded the music of Gurdjieff/deHartmann. See: www.melaniemonsour.com

Chapter 4

- If you have a singing bowl, or if you are a musician, you may wish to make your own sounds/music for this practice. If you are making your own sound, it works best to choose something familiar enough that all your focus doesn't have to go into playing/singing. The goal is to be immersed in the sound itself.

- Track 1 on the accompanying CD contains five minutes of suitable chant music. Track 4 is a timed silence of five minutes duration.
- For more on toning see www.vocalmeditation.blogspot.com
- *The Spirituality of Music* by John Bird is a celebration of music and some of the many ways it can be transformative. (John Bird, *The Spirituality of Music*, Kelowna, BC: Wood Lake Publishing Inc., 2008)

Chapter 5

Matthew Fox, *Creativity: Where the Divine and the Human Meet*, (New York: Tarcher Penguin, 2002).

Lois Huey-Heck and Jim Kalnin, *The Spirituality of Art*, Northstone (an imprint of Wood Lake Publishing) Kelowna, BC, 2006.

The practice of deep-seeing is inspired by the work of the visionary artist, author, and spiritual seeker Frederick Franck, who lived and created well into his nineties. In his phenomenal, best-selling book *The Zen of Seeing: Seeing/Drawing as Meditation*, Franck wrote, "…this Seeing/Drawing (is) a way of meditation, a way of getting into intimate touch with the visible world around us…" May it be so.

For flexibility, portability and economy I use a 100-page, metal coil-bound sketchbook (5.5" by 8.5") as journal and sketchbook in one.

For somewhat larger works I like a 8.5" × 11" metal coil-bound book with much heavier paper that will handle more water and more layering.

Chapter 6

Gabrielle Roth has written several books and has created/recorded many DVDs and about 20 audio recordings to inspire and support people in this practice. For decades she has been helping people experience and integrate these archetypal energy patterns – bringing us to more wholeness and ever-deeper communion with our true selves, with each other, with all life forms and with God.

It's worth searching out Gabrielle Roth online for the You Tube videos of her and her work (sifting through some rather… interesting "other stuff"). You can also learn more and find her resources at her own website www.gabrielleroth.com.

The audio guide for the Five Elements tai ji practice is track 8 on the accompanying CD.

Chapter 7

The chant *Be Still and Know That I Am God* is track 9 on the accompanying CD. I first learned it from Lynn Baumon.

Tracks 4, 7, and 10 contain five-, ten- and 20-minute periods of silence respectively.

Chapter 8

Texts for Lectio Divina
An Evolutionary Covenant
I will be your God, if you will be my people. I have come to you in many forms, and will continue to be present to you in radiant diversity and beauty. My people will never stop growing, because I manifest anew each

moment. If you remain open to my presence in new discoveries, and continue to evolve – loving diversity, growing in mind, heart and body, and loving wisdom – I will be your God. Learn from other creatures the sacred intelligence of the universe. These creatures are your kin. I will be with you in the tumult of change, giving you the courage, the power, and the wisdom to endure and celebrate transformation.

> – From *Darwin, Divinity and the Dance of the Cosmos* by Bruce Sanguin. Used with permission.

An Alternative Lord's Prayer
Loving Presence, luminous in all creation,
Hallowed be your name.
Thy kin-dom come.
May we reflect on earth
the yielding perfection of the heavens.
Help us to receive an illumined measure
   from the earth this day.
Forgive us when we trespass against others,
human and other-than-human,
as we forgive others who trespass against us.
Keep us on the path of wisdom
when we are tempted to take the selfish
   path.
May it be your rule we follow,
your power we exercise,
and your radiance that allures.

May this be the truth that guides our lives,
the ground from which our future will grow,
until we meet again.

> – From *Darwin, Divinity and the Dance of the Cosmos* by Bruce Sanguin. Used with permission.

Psalm 122 (excerpt)
From all over the world,
many feet beat a path to the holy places.
They struggle over high mountain passes;
They shuffle across dusty deserts;
They crawl along the walls of river canyons.
Straggling lines of searchers converge in a
   fertile valley;
A great shout of joy goes up to the heavens.
Muslims, Christians, Jews, Hindus – in
   common cause
the great religions rise above doctrinal
   differences.
Pray for their unity;
pray for their commitment.
May they generate peace among their
   peoples.

> – From *Everyday Psalms* by James Taylor. Used with permission.

Why Pray?

…St. Augustine once said, "You have us for yourself; and our hearts are restless until they find their rest in you." Prayer, then, is a deep soul conversation with the Divine, an intimacy with Ultimacy…As the Buddha pointed out, the true cause of suffering in the world is the host of our desires, our graspings, our wants. Like Christ, he taught that if the lower ego with its "grasping at" or "attachment to" physical realities can be (brought into service of the Holy) much of the inevitable suffering can be avoided or reduced greatly. To say, "I shall not want," then, clearly doesn't mean every petty wish or ephemeral desire will be granted. It means instead that nothing essential to our… final peace… will ever be lacking in this life or beyond.

– From *Prayer: The Hidden Fire* by Tom Harpur. Used with permission.

Chapter 9

Pema Chodron; *Meditation for Difficult Times: Awakening Compassion through the Practice of Tonglen*, Sounds True, Denver, Colorado.

BIBLIOGRAPHY

Coleman Barks with John Moyne, *The Essential Rumi* (New York: HarperSanFrancisco, 1995).

Thomas Berry, *The Great Work: Our Way into the Future* (New York: Bell Tower, 1999).

Therese Bertherat with Carol Bernstein, *The Body Has Its Reasons: Self-Awareness Through Conscious Movement* (Rochester: Healing Arts Press, 1989).

Cynthia Bourgeault, *Mystical Hope: Trusting in the Mercy of God* (Cambridge: Cowley, 2001).

Cynthia Bourgeault, *The Wisdom Way of Knowing: Reclaiming an Ancient Tradition to Awaken the Heart* (San Francisco: Jossey Bass, 2003).

Barbara Brown Taylor, *An Altar in the World: A Geography of Faith* (New York: Harper One, 2009).

Pema Chodron, *Practicing Peace in Times of War: Where the divine and the human meet* (Boston: Shambhala, 2006).

Andrew Harvey, *A Walk with Four Spiritual Guides: Krishna, Buddha, Jesus, and Ramakrishna,* (Woodstock VT: Skylight Paths/Jewish Lights, 2003).

Kabir Edmund Helminski, *Living Presence: A Sufi Way to Mindfulness & the Essential Self* (New York: Tarcher Putnam, 1992).

Abraham Joshua Heschel, *The Sabbath* (New York: Farrar Straus and Giroux, 1951).

Nan C. Merrill, *Psalms for Praying: An Invitation to Wholeness* (New York: Continuum, 2006).

Thich Nhat Hanh, *You Are Here: Discovering the Magic of the Present Moment* (Boston: Shambhala, 2009).

Thich Nhat Hanh, *The Energy of Prayer* (Berkeley: Parallax Press, 2006).

Thich Nhat Hanh, Thich and Ngyuen Anh-Huong, *Walking Meditation* (Denver: Sounds True, 2006).

Gunilla Norris, *Inviting Silence: Universal Principles of Meditation* (New York: Bluebridge, 2004).

John O'Donohue, *Anam Cara: A Book of Celtic Wisdom* (New York: Harper Perennial, 1998).

John O'Donohue, *To Bless the Space Between Us: A Book of Blessings* (New York: Doubleday, 2008).

Paul Pearsall, *The Heart's Code: Tapping the Wisdom and Power of Our Heart Energy, The New Findings About Cellular Memories and Their Role in the Mind/Body/Spirit Connection* (New York, Broadway Books, 1998).

Gabrielle Roth, *Sweat Your Prayers: Movement as Spiritual Practice* (New York: Jeremy P. Tarcher, 1997).

Donna Schaper, *Sabbath Keeping* (Cambridge: Cowley, 1999).

David Steindl-Rast, and Sharon Lebell, *Music of Silence* (Berkeley: Seastone, 1998).

Arlene Stepputat, *The Caring Heart* (Santa Barbara: Blue Point Books, 2004).

Eckhart Tolle, *Stillness Speaks* (Novato: New World Library, 2003).

Macrina Wiederkehr, *Seven Sacred Pauses: Living Mindfully Through the Hours of the Day* (Notre Dame: Sorin Books, 2008).

Cynthia Winton-Henry with Phil Porter, *What the Body Wants* (Kelowna: Northstone, 2004).